TRAVELS IN INDIA

TRAVELS IN INDIA

DURING

The Years

1780, 1781, 1782, & 1783.

by

WILLIAM HODGES, R.A.

GYAN

Published by

Gyan Publishing House
5, Ansari Road
Daryaganj, New Delhi-110002
Phone: 011-47034999, 9811692060
E-mail: books@gyanbooks.com

Distribution Network
gyanbooks.com
India, USA, Canada, UK, Australia, France

ISBN : 978-81-212-2577-9 (PB)
First Published, 1793

2nd Impression 2021

Printed at: Gyan Press, Delhi.

Travels in India
Author: William Hodges

TRAVELS

IN

INDIA,

DURING

THE YEARS

1780, 1781, 1782, & 1783.

BY WILLIAM HODGES, R. A.

LONDON:

PRINTED FOR THE AUTHOR,

AND SOLD BY J. EDWARDS, PALL-MALL.

MDCCXCIII.

TABLE of the PLATES,

WITH

DIRECTIONS TO THE BINDER.

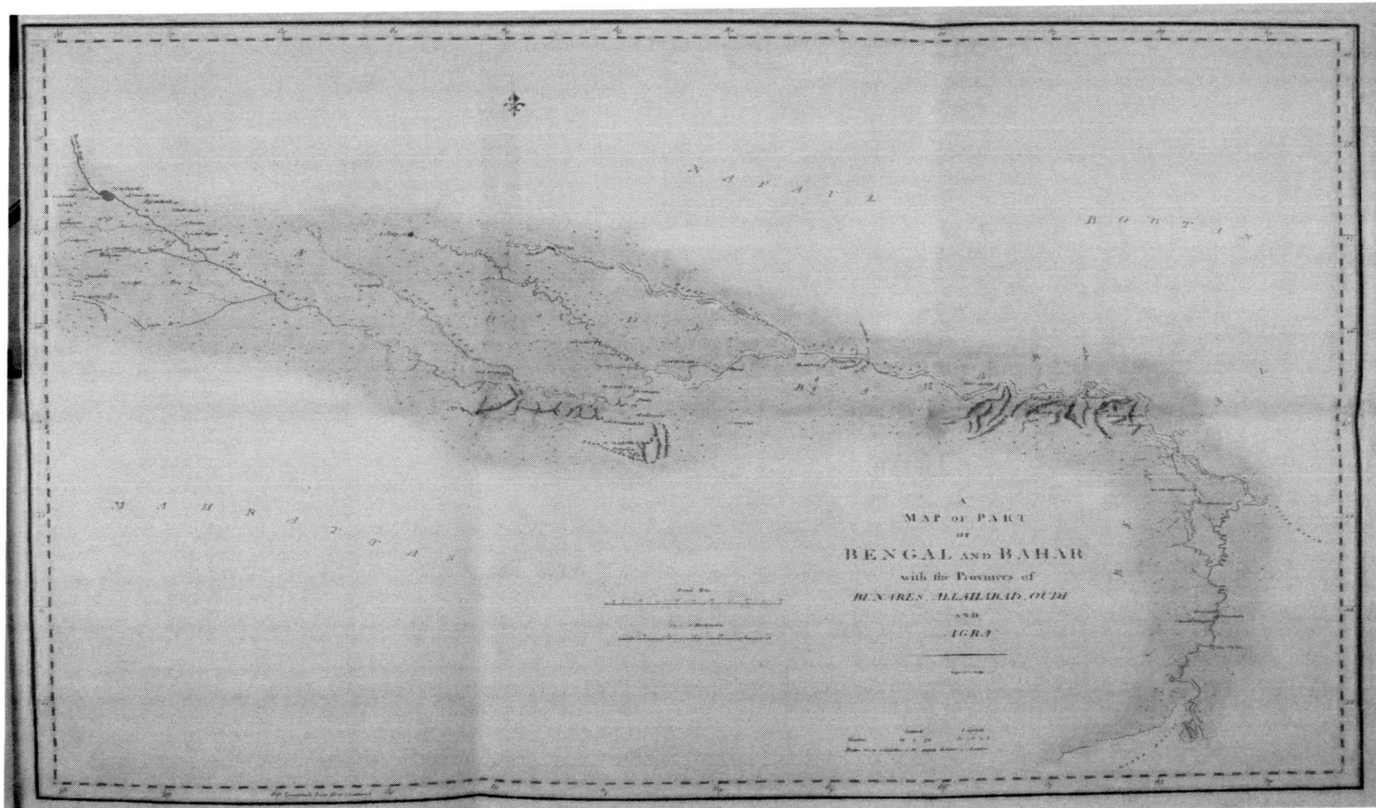
A
MAP OF PART
OF
BENGAL AND BAHAR
with the Provinces of
BENARES, ALLAHABAD, OUDH
AND
AGRA
NAPAUL
BOOTAN
MAHRATTAS

PREFACE.

THE intimate connexion which has ſo long ſubſiſted between this country and the continent of India, naturally renders every Engliſhman deeply intereſted in all that relates to a quarter of the globe which has been the theatre of ſcenes highly important to his country; and which, perhaps, at the moment when he peruſes the deſcription of it, may be the reſidence or the grave of ſome of his deareſt friends.

IT is only matter of ſurprize, that, of a country ſo nearly allied to us, ſo little ſhould be known. The public is, indeed, greatly indebted to the learned labours of gentlemen, who have reſided there, for the information which they have afforded concerning the Laws and the Religion of the Hindoo tribes; as well as for correct and well digeſted details of the tranſactions of the Mogul government. But of the face of the country, of its arts, and natural productions, little has yet been said. Gentlemen who have resided long in India lose the idea of the first impression which that very curious country makes upon an entire stranger: the novelty is soon effaced, and the mind, by a common and natural operation, soon directs its views to more abstract speculation; reasoning assumes the place of observation, and the traveller is lost in the philosopher.

To supply, in some slight degree, this hiatus in the topographical department of literature, is the immediate object of the following pages. It will, I flatter myself, not be disagreeable to my readers to be informed, that they consist of a few plain observations, noted down upon the spot, in the simple garb of truth, without the smallest embellishment from fiction, or from fancy. They were chiefly intended for my own amusement, and to enable me to explain to my friends a number of drawings which I had made during my residence in India, some of which accompany the present publication. The apology is trite; but in this case its truth, and the respectability of the name to which I refer, must plead my excuse......it was owing entirely to the influence and persuasion of my most justly esteemed friend, Henry James Pye, Esq. Poet Laureat, that these observations have been submitted to a tribunal, which I have ever regarded with awful respect......THE PUBLIC.

While I acknowledge my heart-felt obligations to one friend, it is not conſiſtent with my preſent feelings to omit the kind attentions of another. My learned friend, Dr. Gregory, by his peruſal and reviſion of my manuſcript, contributed greatly to leſſen my apprehenſions of that ordeal to which I was about to commit myſelf; and though he inſiſts upon my ſtating, that his corrections were almoſt entirely verbal, yet I cannot but be conſcious, that, without them, the work would have appeared in a ſtill more imperfect ſtate.

After all, I am aware that I ſtand in need of every candid allowance on the part of my readers. It is evident that the ſtudies abſolutely requiſite to any degree of proficiency in a liberal art, and the practice of that art afterwards as a profeſſion, can leave but little leiſure for the cultivation of literature; and perhaps my engagements have been even more unfavourable to this object than thoſe of moſt artiſts. A long circumnavigation, and the profeſſional labour required in completing the works for Captain Cook's ſecond voyage, occupied me for ſeveral years; and a voyage to India, with my different excurſions in that country, abſorbed no inconſiderable portion of my time and attention.

On another part of this work I can ſpeak with rather more confidence, becauſe I am leſs perſonally concerned; and becauſe, as far as I am concerned, I appear in my proper profeſſional character. The drawings, from which the plates for this work are engraved, I have already mentioned were made upon the ſpot: and, to the utmoſt of my ability, are fair and accurate repreſentations of the originals. Of the execution of the plates, while I feel that too much cannot be ſaid, my ſenſes ſufficiently convince me that it is unneceſſary to ſay any thing. I therefore conclude with ſhortly returning my thanks to the artiſts for the care and attention they have beſtowed upon them.

QUEEN STREET, May Fair,
Feb. 18, 1793.

TRAVELS

IN

INDIA.

CHAP. I.

General Appearance of the Coaſt—Of the Town of Madras—Boats of the Country—Firſt Reception of a Stranger—His Senſations on entering the Country—War with Hyder Ally—General Diſtreſs—Deſcriptive Sketch of the Country, Buildings, &c.—Indian Temple.

THE whole extent of the Coaſt of Coromandel is an even, low, ſandy country; and about Madras the land riſes ſo little and ſo gradually from the ſea, that the ſpectator is ſcarcely able to mark the diſtinction, till he is aſſiſted by the appearance of the different objects which preſent themſelves upon the ſhore.

THE Engliſh town, riſing from within Fort St. George, has from the ſea a rich and beautiful appearance; the houſes being covered with a ſtucco called chunam, which in itſelf is nearly as compact as the fineſt marble, and, as it bears as high a poliſh, is equally ſplendid with that elegant material. The ſtile of the buildings is in general handſome. They conſiſt of long colonades, with open porticoes, and flat roofs, and offer to the eye an appearance ſimilar to what we may conceive of a Grecian city in the age of Alexander. The clear, blue, cloudleſs ſky, the poliſhed white buildings, the bright ſandy beach, and the dark green ſea, preſent a combination totally new to the eye of an Engliſhman, juſt arrived from London, who, accuſtomed to the ſight of rolling maſſes of clouds floating in a damp atmoſphere, cannot but contemplate the difference with delight: and the eye being thus gratified, the mind ſoon aſſumes a gay and tranquil habit, analogous to the pleaſing objects with which it is ſurrounded.

Some time before the ſhip arrives at her anchoring ground, ſhe is hailed by the boats of the country filled with people of buſineſs, who come in crowds on board. This is the moment in which an European feels the great diſtinction between Aſia and his own country. The ruſtling of fine linen, and the general hum of unuſual converſation, preſents to his mind for a moment the idea of an aſſembly of females. When he aſcends upon the deck, he is ſtruck with the long muſlin dreſſes,* and black faces † adorned with very large gold ear-rings and white turbans. The firſt ſalutation he receives from theſe ſtrangers is by bending their bodies very low, touching the deck with the back of the hand, and the forehead three times.

THE natives firſt ſeen in India by an European voyager, are Hindoos, the original inhabitants of the Peninſula. In this part of India they are delicately framed, their hands ‡ in particular are more like thoſe of tender females; and do not appear to be, what is conſidered a proper proportion to the reſt of the perſon, which is uſually above the middle ſize. Correſpondent to this deli-

* THIS dreſs is in India uſually worn both by Hindoos and Mahomedans, and is called Jammah; whence the dreſs well known in England, and worn by children, is uſually called a jam.

† THE complexions of the people on the Coaſt of Coromandel and to the ſouthward, are conſiderably darker than thoſe to the northward. It is alſo to be obſerved, that the native Hindoos are generally darker than the Muſſulman, who originally came from Tartary and Perſia. The latter may in fact be called a fair people; and I have even ſeen many of them with red hair and florid complexions. It is a well known fact, that when a Tartar or Perſian family has reſided in India for a few generations, their complexions have conſiderably deepened. The Mogul family of the houſe of Timoor, I underſtand, are of a deep olive complexion.

‡ IT has been obſerved of the arms frequently brought to this country, that the gripe of the ſabre is too ſmall for moſt European hands.

cacy of appearance are their manners, mild, tranquil, and ſeduloufly attentive: in this laſt reſpect they are indeed remarkable, as they never interrupt any perſon who is ſpeaking, but wait patiently till he has concluded; and then anſwer with the moſt perfect reſpect and compoſure.

From the ſhip a ſtranger is conveyed on ſhore in a boat of the country, called a Maſſoolah boat: a work of curious conſtruction, and well calculated to elude the violent ſhocks of the ſurf, that breaks here with great violence: they are formed without a keel, flat bottomed, with the ſides raiſed high, and ſewed together with the fibres of the cocoa-nut tree, and caulked with the ſame material: they are remarkably light, and are managed with great dexterity by the natives: they are uſually attended by two kattamarans, (rafts) paddled by one man each, the intention of which is, that, ſhould the boat be overſet by the violence of the ſurf, the perſons in it may be preſerved. The boat is driven, as the ſailors ſay, high and dry; and the paſſengers are landed on a fine, ſandy beach: and immediately enter the fort of Madras.

The appearance of the natives is exceedingly varied, ſome are wholly naked, and others ſo clothed, that nothing but the face and neck is to be diſcovered; beſides this, the European is ſtruck at firſt with many other objects, ſuch as women carried on men's ſhoulders on pallankeens, and men riding on horfeback clothed in linen dreffes like women: which, united with the very different face of the country from all he had ever feen or conceived of, excite the ftrongeft emotions of furprife!

It is impoffible to defcribe the enthufiafm with which I felt myfelf actuated on this occafion; all that I faw filled my mind with expectations of what was yet unfeen. I prepared therefore eagerly for a tour through the country; but my route was fcarcely fixed, when I was interrupted by the great fcourge of human nature, the great enemy of the arts, war, which, with horrors perhaps unknown to the civilized regions of Europe, defcended like a torrent over the whole face of the country, driving the peaceful hufbandman from his plow, and the manufacturer from his loom. On the eighteenth day of July, 1780, I was a melancholy witnefs to its effects, the multitude coming in from all quarters to Madras as a place of refuge, bearing on their fhoulders the fmall remains of their little property, mothers with infants at their breafts, fathers leading their horfes burthened with their young families, others fitting on the miferable remains of their fortunes on a hackery,* and dragged through the duft by weary bullocks: every object was marked by confufion and difmay, from the 18th to the 21ft, the numbers

* A hackery is a fmall covered carriage upon two wheels, drawn by bullocks, and ufed generally for the female part of the family.

daily increafing: and it was fuppofed that within the fpace of three days not lefs than two hundred thoufand of the country people were received within the *black town of Madras. Our Government behaved on this melancholy occafion with their ufual humanity and liberality; and not only publick, but private relief was afforded them to a confiderable amount.

THOSE poor people were foon afterwards diftributed to the northward, and into the fircars; which are lands that lay to the northward of Madras, and but of late years ceded to the Englifh Government.

MR. Smith was at this period at the head of the Government of Madras: and the folicitous attention of his lady, to relieve the private inconvenience of many Englifh families, who were alfo obliged to take fhelter within the walls of the fort, muft ever be remembered with refpect.

EVERY object that now prefented itfelf to the imagination bore the fame threatening and calamitous afpect: the country houfes of the Englifh, within one mile of the fort, were ftripped of their furniture, by the owners, even

* Adjoining the glacis of Fort St. George, to the northward, is a large town, commonly called the Black town, and which is fortified fufficiently to prevent any furprife by a body of horfe.

to the doors and window-blinds; this indeed was no more than neceſſary, as the enemy extended their depredations even to the walls of Madras; and no ſecurity could be found without the fort; until the camp was formed at the Mount, a place about ten Engliſh miles weſt of Madras. Every gentleman now poſſeſſing a houſe within the fort, was happy in accommodating the family of his friend; who before had reſided on Choultry plain.*

THE troops being collected from different quarters, with proviſions and a proper train of artillery, the vanquiſhed ſpirits of the people appeared to revive; and the reyot was again ſeen cultivating his rice fields, or collecting the fruits. Nothing leſs was expected when the army took the field, but that Hyder Ally would very ſoon be eſcorted by a party of our troops into Fort St. George, and there make a public atonement for the miſeries he had occaſioned. This viſion ſoon vaniſhed, in the unhappy fate of Colonel Baillie's detachment, and the return

* THE country near Madras is a perfect flat, on which is built, at a ſmall diſtance from the fort, a ſmall Choultry: theſe are publick buildings found all over Hindoſtan, and are of Hindoo origin; they are in fact analogous to thoſe buildings called caravanſerais, well known through Aſia. They have been erected and endowed by the liberality of princes, or the benevolence and piety of individuals. A Bramin generally attends them who adminiſters relief to the poor and diſtreſſed, who are frequently ſupplied alſo with a matt to lie on, tanks, or reſervoirs of water, or wells, are commonly near them.

of the army from a three week's campaign, reduced in its numbers and dispirited by its losses. These circumstances are too strongly marked in the page of history to make it necessary to recount their particulars in a descriptive work like this. The arrival of Sir Eyre Coote from Bengal, with money and other supplies, in September, and the active measures pursued by that gallant officer, restored confidence to the troops; and the most sanguine hopes of the inhabitants from his exertions were not disappointed.

The opportunities that offer to a painter are few, in a country which is over-run by an active enemy. I made however among others a drawing of Marmalong bridge, which is a very modern work, built, as I am informed, at the private expence of an Armenian merchant. It is over a small river that runs near the mount, and falls into the sea at a little distance before the village of St. Thomá, four miles to the southward of Madras. The Portugueze had formerly a considerable settlement at this village. The church and the dwelling-houses of a few Portugueze families yet remain here. The legendary tale of the Roman Catholic church is, that St. Thomas the apostle, in the course of his mission to India, suffered martyrdom on the spot where the church is built.

The settlement of Madras was formed by the English at or about the middle of the last century, and was a place of no real conſequence, but for its trade, until the war ſo ably carried on by General Stringer Lawrence, from the years 1748 to 1752; and which originated from the claims of Chunda Saib, in oppoſition to our ally Mahomed Ally Cawn, the preſent Nabob of Arcot; from which period the Engliſh may be conſidered as Sovereigns. In the ſchool of this able officer the late Lord Clive received his military education.

Fort St. George, or Madras, riſes, as has been already intimated, from the margin of the ſea, and is allowed by the ableſt engineers to be a place of conſiderable ſtrength. It was planned by the ingenious Mr. Robins, the author of Lord Anſon's Voyages, who was eminent for his general and philoſophical, as well as for his mathematical knowledge. Since his time many works have been added.

In Fort St. George are many handſome and ſpacious ſtreets. The houſes may be conſidered as elegant, and particularly ſo from the beautiful material with which they are finiſhed, the chunam. The inner apartments are not highly decorated, preſenting to the eye only white walls; which, however, from the marble-like appearance of the ſtucco, give a freſhneſs grateful in ſo hot a country. Ceilings are very uncommon in the rooms. Indeed it is impoſſible to find any which will reſiſt the ravages of that deſtructive inſect the white ant. Theſe animals are chiefly formidable from the immenſity of their numbers, which are ſuch as to deſtroy, in one night's time, a ceiling of any dimenſions. I ſaw an inſtance in the ceiling to the portico of the Admiralty, or Governor's houſe, which fell in flakes of twenty feet ſquare. It is the wood work which ſerves for the baſis of the ceilings, ſuch as the laths, beams, &c. that theſe inſects attack; and this will ſerve to explain the circumſtance I have juſt mentioned.

THE houſes on Choultry plain are many of them beautiful pieces of architecture, the apartments ſpacious and magnificent. I know not that I ever felt more delight, than in going on a viſit to a family on Choultry plain, ſoon after my arrival at Madras, in the cool of the evening, after a very hot day. The moon ſhone in its fulleſt luſtre, not a cloud overcaſt the ſky, and every houſe on the plain was illuminated. Each family, with their friends, were in the open porticoes, enjoying the breeze. Such a ſcene appears more like a tale of enchantment than a reality, to the imagination of a ſtranger juſt arrived.

THERE are few objects to be met with here, which ſerve to illuſtrate the hiſtory or characters of the original inhabitants of India. One, however, is too curious to be omitted, and that is a beautiful Hindoo Temple, or Pagoda, at Triplecane, two miles ſouth of Madras. It is of conſiderable magnitude; and the top of the building riſing conſiderably above the trees, it is ſeen all over the country. Adjoining to the temple is a large tank, with ſteps deſcending to the bottom, filled with water. The whole is of ſtone, and the maſonry excellent. On the ſurface of the temple are many baſſo relievos, which I ſuppoſe to relate to the religion of the Hindoos; but whether they are connected with the rites and worſhip of Bramah or not, I am not able to ſay: for ſome of them are of the moſt indecent kind. I made an accurate drawing of this building, which was ſent to England, and loſt on board the General Barker Eaſt Indiaman, when that ſhip was wrecked on the coaſt of Holland, in 1781; but as I have made drawings of other Hindoo temples, I leſs lament the loſs. The annexed plate, a view of the great Pagoda at Tanjore, is from a picture which I painted from an accurate drawing made by Mr. Topping, an ingenious friend of mine, now on a ſurvey of the coaſt of Coromandel for the Hon. the Eaſt India Company, and will ſerve to give the reader a general idea of theſe efforts of Indian architecture.

A VIEW of the GREAT PAGODA at TANJORE.

Engraved by T. Maitland from a picture Painted by W. Hodges R.A. in the Collection of Warren Hastings Esq.

London Published by T. Edwards Pall Mall, Jan. 1, 1793.

CHAP. II.

Voyage to Bengal—Description of the Fort and Town of Calcutta—Route from Calcutta to the Plains of Plassey—Description of that memorable Spot—The Author's Progress through the Country—Ruins of a Zananah—Cataract of Mootejerna—Happiness of India—Description of Bauglepoor—Town and Fort of Mongheir—Remarks on the Mode of travelling in India—Voyage back to Calcutta on the Ganges—Temples—Females bathing—Singular Appearance by Night.

AFTER residing a year at Madras, as no prospect presented itself of seeing and making drawings in the interior part of the country, I determined to pursue my voyage to Bengal: and as I found my health on the decline, I entertained thoughts of returning to Europe by the following season. I embarked in February, 1781, and arrived in the Ganges in March. A change of air and a sea voyage frequently produces a happy alteration in the constitutions of valetudinarians in India; and I accordingly found that on my arrival in Bengal my health was perfectly re-established.

THE appearance of the country on the entrance of the Ganges, or Houghly River (this being only a branch of the

Great Ganges) is rather unpromiſing; a few buſhes at the water's edge, forming a dark line, juſt marking the diſtinction between ſky and water, are the only objects to be ſeen. As the ſhip approaches Calcutta the river narrows; that which is called the Garden Reach, preſents a view of handſome buildings, on a flat ſurrounded by gardens: theſe are villas belonging to the opulent inhabitants of Calcutta. The veſſel has no ſooner gained one other reach of the river than the whole city of Calcutta burſts upon the eye. This capital of the Britiſh dominions in the Eaſt is marked by a conſiderable fortreſs, on the ſouth ſide of the river, which is allowed to be, in ſtrength and correctneſs of deſign, ſuperior to any in India. On the fore ground of the picture is the water-gate of the fort, which reflects great honour on the talents of the engineer—the ingenious Colonel Polier. The glacis and eſplanade are ſeen in perſpective, bounded by a range of beautiful and regular buildings; and a conſiderable reach of the river, with veſſels of various claſſes and ſizes, from the largeſt Indiamen to the ſmalleſt boat of the country, cloſes the ſcene. A plate, repreſenting this view, from a picture taken on the ſpot, and admirably engraved by Mr. Byrne, an artiſt whoſe reputation is not to be raiſed by any eulogium in this place, is annexed.

A EUROPEAN lands here in the midſt of a great city, without paſſing the outer draw-bridges of a fort: here are no centinels with the keen eye of ſuſpicion, no ſtoppage of

A VIEW of CALCUTTA, taken from FORT WILLIAM.

Engraved by W. Byrne from a Picture Painted by W. Hodges R.A. in the Collection of Warren Hastings Esq.r

London, Published by J. Edwards, Pall Mall, Jan 1st 1793.

baggage. The hoſpitality which a ſtranger experiences from the inhabitants, and particularly from thoſe to whom he is recommended, correſponds exactly with the freedom of his admiſſion into the city; and the kindneſs which I experienced on this occaſion from my much lamented friend Henry Davies, Eſq. late Advocate General of Bengal, can never be forgotten.

The city of Calcutta extends from the Weſtern point of Fort William, along the banks of the river, almoſt to the village of Coſſipoor: that is about four and a half Engliſh miles. The breadth in many parts is inconſiderable. The ſtreets are broad; the line of buildings, ſurrounding two ſides of the eſplanade of the fort, is magnificent; and it adds greatly to the ſuperb appearance, that the houſes are detached from each other, and inſulated in a great ſpace. The buildings are all on a large ſcale, from the neceſſity of having a free circulation of air, in a climate the heat of which is extreme. The general approach to the houſes is by a flight of ſteps, with great projecting porticoes, or ſurrounded by colonades or arcades, which give them the appearance of Grecian temples; and indeed every houſe may be conſidered as a temple dedicated to hoſpitality.

Calcutta, from a ſmall and inconſiderable fort, which yet remains (and in which is the famous black-hole, ſo fatal to many of our countrymen in 1756), and a few warehouſes, was ſoon raiſed to a great and opulent city, when the government of the kingdom of Bengal fell into the hands of the Engliſh. For its magnificence, however, it is indebted ſolely to the liberal ſpirit and excellent taſte of the late Governor General; and it muſt be confeſſed, that the firſt houſe was raiſed by Mr. Haſtings which deſerves the name of a piece of architecture: in fact, it is even in a purer ſtyle than any that has been built ſince, although it is on a ſmaller ſcale than many others.

THE mixture of European and Aſiatic manners, which may be obſerved in Calcutta, is curious:—coaches, phætons, ſingle horſe chaiſes, with the pallankeens and hackeries of the natives—the paſſing ceremonies of the Hindoos—the different appearances of the fakirs—form a ſight perhaps more novel and extraordinary than any city in the world can preſent to a ſtranger. Some views in the city of Calcutta, publiſhed by Mr. Daniel, are highly to be commended for their accuracy.

A FEW weeks after my arrival in Bengal, an opportunity offered itſelf, which I immediately embraced, to make drawings of part of the country, as high as Mongheir, on the Ganges, a diſtance of three hundred Engliſh miles; and I proceeded on this journey in the middle of the month of April following, by dauk bearers (in a pallankeen) or pallankeen carriers. Theſe are perſons hired by government, and fixed at the ſeveral ſtages or poſts for facilitating travelling: each ſtage, on an average, may be ten Engliſh miles. The number of perſons are uſually nine, with two additional men or boys, to carry baggage and lights in the night, called moſſoljees, from the name of the lights, moſſol.

FROM the apparent ſtate of a country, a juſt eſtimate may generally be formed of the happineſs or the miſery of a people. Where there is neatneſs in the cultivation of the land, and that land tilled to the utmoſt of its boundaries, it may reaſonably be ſuppoſed that the government is the protector and not the oppreſſor of the people. Throughout the kingdom of Bengal it appears highly flouriſhing in tillage of every kind, and abounding in cattle. The villages are neat and clean, and filled with ſwarms of people.

THERE are few objects to attract the attention of the curious traveller from Calcutta, until he reaches the plains of Plaſſey. This ſpot to every reflecting Engliſhman muſt be highly intereſting, when he conſiders that on this theatre, in the month of June, 1757, was diſputed the exiſtence of his countrymen in Bengal, even as merchants. The great abilities diſplayed by Lord Clive previous to the battle of Plaſſey, as well as in that action, both as a general and a politician, undoubtedly entitle him to the high reputation which is attached to his memory; ſince on that plain was laid the foundation of an empire in India, the influence of which has extended over a larger tract of country, and greater numbers of people, than have been united under any one government since the time of Aurungzebe.

At Plassey is a house which was once a hunting seat of the Nabob of Bengal: it is distant from Calcutta about seventy English miles, and somewhat more than thirty from Moorshedabad. In Moorshedabad there are few buildings of note: the most considerable is the remains of the Cutterah. This was formerly a publick seminary for men of learning among the Musselmans; but it has long since gone to decay. It consists of a large square area, each side of which is somewhat more than seventy feet in length, surrounded by a cloyster, divided into single rooms, crowned with a dome, and one window in each. In the center on the side opposite the entrance was a mosque, raised considerably above the buildings on either side: the extreme angles on that side where the mosque was situated are terminated by two towers, rising several feet higher than the rest of the building.

This building was erected by Jaffier Cawn, the Nabob of Bengal, in the early part of the present century; who, from the mildness of his manners, his love of learning, and strict attention to justice, was the most popular nobleman who ever held that office in Bengal under the Mogul government. Moorshedabad was the seat of his residence, and to this place he invited men of talents. On the opposite ſide of the river is the tomb of Aliverdi Cawn, the grandfather of Suraja Dowlah, ſo well known for his hatred to the Engliſh, and his conduct to his priſoners on the taking of Calcutta in 1756.* This is an oblong building,

* When the fort of Calcutta was cloſely beſieged by Suraja Dowlah, Mr. Drake, the governor, and many others, with ſeveral ladies of the ſettlement, eſcaped to the Engliſh ſhips then lying off the town, and which ſhips fell down as low as Fulta, one third of the diſtance to the mouth of the river, where they remained for ſeven months in the greateſt diſtreſs, both for proviſions and every other article of neceſſaries. Mr. Gregory, a gentleman ſince well known in the political world, and particularly for his knowledge in India affairs, and many years a Director of the Eaſt India Company in London, ventured in a very heavy gale of wind, in a country boat, to paſs Calcutta, and proceeded to Chardenagore, to ſolicit aſſiſtance from the French governor, who received him with all the perſonal politeneſs that is the mark of that nation, but without offering any thing to remove the diſtreſs of the Engliſh at Fulta. From the French Mr. Gregory proceeded to the Dutch ſettlement at Chinſurah, where he was received with unaffected good manners and friendlineſs. After relating the diſtreſſes his countrymen laboured under, the Dutch governor prepared for their relief; and his lady went round the ſettlement and procured linen and other articles, for the accommodation and comfort of the ladies; and, in the courſe of two days, the governor diſpatched a ſloop, under the care of Mr. Van Staten, their commander in chief, to the Engliſh, loaded with ſeveral articles of proviſions, many cheſts of wine, and twenty leaguers of arrack, for the uſe of the people. At the ſame time this humanity was ſhewn to the people on board the ſhips, the governor's houſe was ſo filled with the diſtreſſed that had eſcaped from Calcutta, that he and his family were obliged to ſleep on board a budgerow in the river. The name of the Dutch governor, Mr. Adrian Biſdam, muſt ever be remembered by the Engliſh with reſpect.

crowned with five domes; the center one much larger than the others, and the two extremes less than the intermediate. This pyramidal form is usual in all the buildings of the East, whether Moorish or Hindoo: so minutely attentive have they been to this, that a mosque at Chunar, being tried with a cord stretched from the summit of the center building, the cord has been found to touch the extremes at the outer wall that incloses the building. During the usurpation of Aliverdi Cawn, his wars with the Marhattas, who were continually over-running the country, left him little leisure for the embellishment of the city, however he might have been disposed.

THE road proceeds from Moorshedabad through the villages of Jungepoor and Sooty, to Oodooanullah. This road is crossed by several nullahs,† some of which have ferry boats stationed at them, to accommodate the traveller. At the last mentioned place is a bridge, built by Sultan Sujah, the second son of the Emperor Shah Iehan,* who was appointed Subah of the province of Bengal, one hundred and thirty years ago. This is one of the most elegant specimens in architecture of those times; and it has become famous in ours by the victory obtained over the troops of Meer Cossim, in the year 1764, by the late Major Adams. This

† Nullahs are small streams, or brooks.

* The Emperor Shah Iehan began his reign in the year 1627, and reigned thirty-two years. He was deposed by his third son, the famous Allumgire; better known in Europe by the name of Aurungzebe.

victory was facilitated by an accident that happened on the bridge: the carriage of one of the enemy's large pieces of artillery broke down, and stopping the retreat, threw them into confusion. Oodooanullah is two miles from Rajemahel; and Rajemahel is nearly eighty miles from Moorshedabad: it lies on the western bank of the Ganges, which is high and bold, and at the foot of a chain of hills. The situation is esteemed unhealthy, from the forests in its neighbourhood. It was the seat of the government of Bengal, under Sultan Sujah, and it continued to be his residence until he fell in the contest for the empire with his brother Aurungzebe. The numberless ruins found at and in the neighbourhood, evinced his passion for building; and the great extent of many of them affords a proof of his splendor and magnificence. There yet remains a part of the palace: which was supported by vast octangular piers, raised from the edge of the river. The great hall yet remains, with some lesser apartments, as well as the principal gate leading to the palace: these are surrounded by immense masses of ruins. This palace, in the time of Sultan Sujah, was nearly destroyed by fire: the zananah, or that part inhabited by the females of his family, was totally destroyed.

A TRADITION prevails in this part of the country, that more than three hundred women fell a sacrifice to modesty on this occasion; none of them daring to save themselves, from the apprehension of being seen by the men. At a little diſtance from Rajemahel are the ruins of a zananah, which I went from curioſity to inſpect, as they are when inhabited ſacred places; and I was gratified extremely to obſerve the perfect accuracy in the Hindoſtan pictures which repreſent them. The annexed plate is from an old picture of one which I met with in India. It may not be improper to remark, while I am upon this ſubject, that when the Mogul government was in the plenitude of its power, it was an object with the Omrahs, or great Lords of the court, to hold captive in their zananahs even hundreds of females, collected from various quarters of the empire, and particularly ſo from Caſhmire, a country famous for the beauty of its women.* From Rajemahel the publick road continues by the ſide of the river, at the foot of the hills, to the paſs of Sicri Gully, whence it enters the province of Bahar. This paſs, in the time of the Hindoo and Mogul governments was the commanding entrance from Bahar into the kingdom of Bengal, and was formerly fortified with a ſtrong wall and gate, the ruins of which yet remain. What muſt ſhew the inutility of ſuch fortifications, and the wiſdom of the Britiſh government in ſuffering them to go to

* I cannot but here obſerve that, from the cloſe confinement of the Mahomedan women, there reigns in the zananahs a refined ſpirit of intrigue unknown in Europe in the preſent day. Many accounts are to be found of ſuch in the old Spaniſh novels, which may be accounted for from the Spaniards retaining cuſtoms and prejudices eſtabliſhed among them by their Mooriſh conquerors, long after their expulſion in the fifteenth century.

THE PASS of SICRI GULLY from BENGAL entering into the Province of BAHAR.

Engraved by W. Angus from a Picture Painted by W. Hodges R.A. in the Collection of Warren Hastings Esq.r

London, Published by J. Edwards, Pall Mall, Jan.y 1.1793.

decay, is the eaſe with which they are eluded; for, in the year 1742-3, the whole Mahratta army, conſiſting of fifty thouſand men, under Boſchow Pundit, paſſed through the hills above Colgong, and to the ſouth-weſt of this paſs into Bengal. On the top of the hill is a ruined tomb of a Muſſulman ſied, or ſaint. The whole ſcene appeared to me highly picturesque; a plate, therefore, is given of this view, as it marks the general character of this part of the country. At this place I was met by a party of ſeapoys, ſent by my much lamented and revered friend, the late Auguſtus Cleveland, Eſq. then collector of the diſtricts of Rajemahel and Bauglepoor, to eſcort me to the falls of Mootejerna in the hills, about four coſs, or eight Engliſh miles inland from the river. From the height of the hills, theſe caſcades are clearly ſeen, in the time of the rains, the river being then near thirty feet higher than in the dry ſeaſon, and the falls conſiderably increaſed. The road, or rather path, is through the jungles, or woods; and when rain has lately fallen in the hills, the noiſe of the cataract is diſtinctly heard at the diſtance of two Engliſh miles. It conſiſts of two falls, which taken together, the perpendicular height meaſures one hundred and five feet. The water, falling over vaſt maſſes of rocks, is received in a baſon below, and continues running through fragments of the rock, rent from above, until it is loſt in the Ganges. At the bottom of the lower fall is a great hollow cave, which is eaſily entered from either ſide, and the water is ſeen from within, forming part of the arc of a great circle before. In the interior part of this cave, which may be thirty feet from the front of the rock, the baſe appears to be a mixture of rock and charcoal; that is, the interſtices of the rock appear filled with charcoal, and many fragments broken off are compoſed equally of the two materials. For the ſatisfaction of others I brought away with me two large pieces, which I afterwards ſhewed to ſeveral ingenious gentlemen in Calcutta. The place itſelf, it is true, is held in ſuperſtitious veneration by the common people of the country; and it is poſſible ſome religious ceremonies may have paſſed here, but it is ſcarcely probable that any fire uſed in ſuch ceremonies could have produced ſuch effects.

AFTER returning to Sicri Gully, I continued my route acroſs the paſs of Terriagully, from the top of which a beautiful ſcene opens itſelf to the view; namely, the meandering of the river Ganges through the flat country, and glittering through an immenſe plain, highly cultivated, as far as the extent of the horizon, where the eye is almoſt at a loſs to diſcriminate the termination of ſky and land. From the paſs of Terriagully the road continues by the river ſide, opening in extenſive glades, covered with a fine turf, and only interſperſed with woods, conſiſting of timber trees of conſiderable magnitude, which, from the great heat and moiſture in this part of India, (like all other vegetable productions of the country) continue verdant through a great part of the year. After this the road ſkirts the woods, and

A VIEW of the INSIDE of A ZANANAH.

Engraved by W. Skelton from an Indian Painting in the possession of William Hodges R.A.

London, Publish'd by J. Edwards, Pall Mall, Jan.y [illegible]

under great trees, which are filled with a variety of birds of beautiful colours, many of them of the parrot tribe; and, amongſt others, peacocks in abundance, which ſitting on the vaſt horizontal branches, and diſplaying their varied plumage to the ſun, dazzle the eyes of the traveller as he paſſes. In this route many inferior rivers are paſſed, that feed the waters of the Great Ganges, which, at this ſeaſon of the year, are very low; and the ſteepneſs of many of their banks renders the carriage extremely troubleſome to the pallankeen bearers. At Colgong there is a conſiderable ſtream, that falls into the Ganges, which by its continued force, and particularly in the time of the periodical rains, has detached two large rocks, and formed them into iſlands, covered with woods, full ſeventy yards from the ſhore. There is a paſſage between the iſlands and the ſhore filled with ſunken rocks, which form violent eddies. The paſſage is ſometimes only to be effected by ſmall boats; and in the time of the rains is eſteemed exceedingly dangerous. I knew an inſtance in which it had nearly proved fatal.

THE country about Colgong is, I think, the moſt beautiful I have ſeen in India. The waving appearance of the land, its fine turf and detached woods, backed by the extenſive foreſts on the hills, brought to my mind many of the fine parks in England; and its overlooking the Ganges, which has more the appearance of an ocean at this place than of a river, gives the profpect inexpreffible grandeur.

From this place my route was continued to the village of Sultungunge; oppofite to which, in the river, is the fmall ifland of Jangerah, or, according to fome authors, Jehangueery. This ifland is a rock, with a few trees growing from its interftices, and on the top is a fmall hermitage, inhabited by a Hindoo monk. The fituation this holy father has chofen is certainly a proof of his tafte and of his judgment; for, from the top, he has a moft extenfive profpect of the country and river; and in the fummer heats it muft be cooler than any fituation in its neighbourhood. This rock is confidered by the Hindoos as a facred place; and on many parts of it are pieces of fculpture relative to their mythology. I am concerned I cannot pay fo high a compliment to the art of fculpture among the Hindoos as is ufually paid by many ingenious authors who write on the religion of Bramah. Confidering thefe works, as I do, with the eyes of an artift, they are only to be paralleled with the rude effays of the ingenious Indians I have met with in Otaheite, and on other iflands in the South Seas. The time when thefe fculptures were produced I believe is not eafy to afcertain; but thus much is certain, that the more modern works in fculpture of human figures, by the Hindoos, lay claim to very little more merit than the ancient productions. Some ornaments, however, that I have feen on

BANYAN TREE.

Engraved by B. T. Pouncy from a Picture Painted by W. Hodges R.A.
in the Collection of Warren Hastings Esq.r

London, Published by J. Edwards, Pall Mall [illegible]

Hindoo temples are beautifully carved: but of this I ſhall have occaſion to ſpeak hereafter, when I treat of the ſubject of Hindoo architecture.

I PROCEEDED from Sultungunge to Bauglepoor, where my purſuits were promoted with a degree of liberality that peculiarly marked the mind of the gentleman who then governed this diſtrict; and of whom, in common gratitude, I muſt ever ſpeak with veneration and eſteem. At the entrance of the town of Bauglepoor, I made a drawing of a banyan tree, of which a plate is annexed. This is one of thoſe curious productions in nature which cannot fail to excite the attention of the traveller. The branches of this tree having ſhoots depending from them, and taking root, again produce, and become the parents of others. Theſe trees, in many inſtances, cover ſuch an extent of ground, that hundreds of people may take ſhelter under one of them from the ſcorching rays of the ſun. The care that was taken in the government, and the minute attention to the happineſs of the people, rendered this diſtrict, at this time, (1781) a perfect paradiſe. It was not uncommon to ſee the manufacturer at his loom, in the cool ſhade, attended by his friend ſoftening his labour by the tender ſtrains of muſic. There are to be met with in India many old pictures repreſenting ſimilar ſubjects, in the happy times of the Mogul government.

The situation of the Resident's house, built by Mr. Cleveland, is on a very elevated spot: it is on the banks of a nullah, forming a large island, bounded by the Ganges on one side, and the nullah encircling the other: the island is about four miles across. On the other side is a beautiful park-like country, with clumps of great trees, separated by glades; the whole bounded by wood. This place owes its principal beauty to the good taste of Mr. Cleveland.

From Bauglepoor to Mongheir, is between thirty and forty English miles. The roads are good, the country highly cultivated, and the villages neat. Along the side of the road are the burial places of the Mussulmans; for they, like the ancient Greeks, always bury by or near the highways: those of the common people are mounds of earth, covering the whole length of the body, with a small square column at the head, about three feet high, and another, not more than eighteen inches, at the feet: those of superior rank have mausoleums, decorated in proportion to the wealth or munificence of the family. It is a custom with the women of the family to attend these tombs of their friends, or nearest and most valued relations, after sun-set; and it is both affecting and curious to see them proceeding in groups, carrying lamps in their hands, which they place at the head of the tomb: the effect, considered in a picturesque light, is highly beautiful; with that of sentiment, it is delightful. A print of this subject is subjoined.

MAHOMMEDAN WOMEN attending the TOMBS of their Parents, Relatives, or Friends, at NIGHT.

Engraved by William Skelton from a Picture Painted by William Hodges R.A.

London, Publiſhed by J. Edwards, Pall Mall, Jan.y 1. 1793

MONGHEIR is a large Indian town, with an old fort. One ſide of the fort is flanked by the Ganges, and that to the land by a wide and deep ditch. There are three principal gates; one on the ſide next the river, another on the eaſt ſide, and another on the ſouth. That to the eaſt appears to have been very ſtrong: the walls are flanked with ſquare towers, in the old ſtile of caſtles; many ſimilar ruins being now to be found in England. The fort was built in the middle of the laſt century, by Sultan Sujah; but the place is famous for being a military ſtation many centuries back.* The area within the walls of the fort is very conſiderable; it is generally made a ſtation for a part of the Engliſh troops; and there is a houſe here for the commanding officer, built by the late General Goddard.

FROM Calcutta to Mongheir the face of the country is extremely varied. Bengal, however, to the entrance into the province of Bahar, is almoſt a perfect flat, or the riſe is ſo gentle as not to be perceived. The ſoil is rich, conſiſting chiefly of a black earth, intermixt with fine ſand. From Rajemahel it aſſumes a different character; hills are ſeen riſing in many parts into mountains, and covered with immenſe foreſts of timber: the ſoil here is alſo more arid, and the air drier, than in the lower parts of Bengal. The heat

* On this ſpot was found, a few years back, a braſs plate, with a Sanſchrite inſcription of a grant, as early as the firſt century of Chriſtianity.

in the months of March, April, and May, is immoderate; and, until it becomes tempered by the rains that constantly fall in June and July, it is dreadful to the bearers of the pallankeens to travel in the middle of the day: the dust and heat are then, indeed, so intolerable, that they are frequently under the necessity of putting down their burthens, and sheltering themselves beneath the shade of the banyan trees, many of which are found on the road, particularly by the side of wells, or some little choultry on the borders of a tank. The number of these rural accommodations for travellers reflect the highest credit on the care of the old Hindoo and Moorish governments. It is particularly mentioned in the life of the Emperor Shere Shah, that, although a usurper who obtained the empire by the most atrocious acts, he paid the most humane attention to the comforts and accommodations of his people. He caused wells to be dug at every cos, (or two miles) and trees to be planted on the road side. At many of these wells have I halted in my journies. They are, in general, from ten to fourteen feet in diameter, and lined with stone: the masonry excellent; and they are raised from the surface of the ground by a little wall two feet high. I should have remarked that, throughout Bengal and Bahar, the water is excellent. It is extremely pleasant to observe the variety of travellers that are to be met with on the road; either passing along in groups, under the shade of some spreading tree, by the side of the wells or tanks. In one part may be seen the native soldiers, their half pikes sticking

A PEASANT WOMAN
of
HINDOSTAN.

A SEPOY MATCHLOCK MAN.
in the Service of the native
PRINCES of HINDOSTAN.

Drawn from the Life by W. Hodges R.A.

London, Published by J. Edwards, Pall Mall, Jan. 1. 1793.

by their side, and their shields lying by them, with their sabres and matchlocks; in another part is, perhaps, a company of merchants, engaged in calculation, or of devotees in the act of social worship; and in another, the common Hindoo pallankeen bearers baking their bread. This operation is performed in an easy and expeditious manner by these people: they make a small hole in the earth of about a foot in diameter, in which they light a fire, and on the top of the fire they place a flat iron plate, which they always carry with them, and which they support with stones; they mix their flour with a little water, and bake their cakes, which are soon dressed, are very wholesome, and I think not unpalatable. On the whole, I must say, that the simplicity and primitive appearance of these groups delighted me.

It is not uncommon also, in excursions through these parts of the country, to meet with various fakirs, with a more than savage appearance. Sometimes whole families may be seen travelling up and down the country, forming most beautiful picturesque groups; sometimes with camels loaded with goods; some of the party riding on bullocks, the females in hackeries, and the younger part of the company on small horses, brought from the mountains bordering the eastern side of Bengal. These horses are called tanyans, and are mostly pye-bald. The men march on foot, armed with spears and matchlocks: their sabres and shields are flung across their backs. These are certainly valuable subjects for the painter. The lodgings of the traveller in India are the ſerais, or caravanſerais, (or places for the caravans) as they are called in Europe. Many of theſe are in the great roads, and have been erected either by charitable perſons, or at the public expence. The Emperor, whom I have already mentioned for his attention to the public accommodation, built many, from the extremity of Bengal to Lahore. There is a noble building of this kind remaining at Rajemahel, built by Sultan Sujah, when Subah of Bengal. The form is a ſquare of equal ſides; the entrance from the Bengal road is through a large and highly ornamented gate, which alſo poſſeſſes military ſtrength no leſs than beauty. Round the four ſides is a wall about twenty feet high; attached to the wall round the ſides are ſeparate apartments, covered on the top, and open to the center of the area within. In theſe places the traveller lodges his goods, and ſleeps; the area within the ſquare is for the beaſts. Attendant on theſe ſerais are poor people, who furniſh a ſmall bedſtead for the traveller to ſleep on, and who are rewarded by a trifling ſum, amounting to perhaps a penny Engliſh. The Mahomedan is, in general, a generous man compared with the Hindoo on theſe occaſions. Oppoſite the Bengal gate is another in this ſerai; which, however, is nothing more than merely an opening through the wall.

FROM Mongheir I embarked, and returned by water to Calcutta; and here I had an opportunity of obſerving a ſeries of ſcenery perſectly new; the different boats of the country, and the varied ſhores of the Ganges. This immenſe current of water ſuggeſts rather the idea of an ocean than of a river, the general breadth of it being from two to five miles, and in ſome places more. The largeſt boats ſailing up or paſſing down, appear, when in the middle of the ſtream, as mere points, and the eaſtern ſhore only as a dark line marking the horizon. The rivers I have ſeen in Europe, even the Rhine, appear as rivulets in compariſon with this enormous maſs of water. I do not know a more pleaſant amuſement than ſailing down the Ganges in the warm ſeaſon: the air, paſſing over the great reaches of the river many miles in length, is ſo tempered as to feel delightfully refreſhing. After ſun-ſet the boats are generally moored cloſe to the banks, where the ſhore is bold, and near a gunge or market, for the accommodation of the people. It is common, on the banks of the river, to ſee ſmall Hindoo temples, with gauts or paſſages, and flights of ſteps to the river. In the mornings, at or after ſun-riſe, the women bathe in the river; and the younger part, in particular, continue a conſiderable time in the water, ſporting and playing like Naiads or Syrens. To a painter's mind, the fine antique figures never fail to preſent themſelves, when he obſerves a beautiful female form aſcending theſe ſteps from the river, with wet drapery, which perfectly diſplays the whole perſon, and with vaſes on their heads, carrying water to the temples. A ſight no leſs novel or extraordinary, is the Bramins at their oraiſons; perfectly abſtracted, for the time, to every paſſing object, however attractive. Theſe devotees are generally naked, except a ſmall piece of drapery round the middle. A ſurprizing ſpirit of cleanlineſs is to be obſerved among the Hindoos: the ſtreets of their villages are commonly ſwept and watered, and ſand is frequently ſtrewed before the doors of the houſes. The ſimplicity, and perfectly modeſt character, of the Hindoo women, cannot but arreſt the attention of a ſtranger. With downcaſt eye, and equal ſtep, they proceed along, and ſcarcely turn to the right or to the left to obſerve a foreigner as he paſſes, however new or ſingular his appearance. The men are no leſs remarkable for their hoſpitality, and are conſtantly attentive to accommodate the traveller in his wants. During the whole of the journey in my pallankeen, whatever I wanted, as boiling water for my tea, milk, eggs, &c. &c. I never met with impoſition or delay, but always experienced an uncommon readineſs to oblige, and that accompanied with manners the moſt ſimple and accommodating. In perfect oppoſition is the Muſſulman character;—haughty, not to ſay inſolent; irritable, and ferocious. I beg, however, to be underſtood of the lower claſſes; for a Mooriſh gentleman may be conſidered as a perfect model of a well bred man. The Hindoos are chiefly huſbandmen, manufacturers, and merchants, except two tribes—the Rajapoots, who are military, and the Bramins, who are eccleſiaſtics. The Muſſulmans may be claſſed as entirely military, as few of them exerciſe any other employment, except collecting the revenues, which under the Moorish governments have been always done by military force.

At this season of the year it is not uncommon, towards the evening, to see a small black cloud rising in the eastern part of the horizon, and afterwards spreading itself to the north-west. This phenomenon is always attended with a violent storm of wind, and flashes of the strongest and most vivid lightning and heavy thunder, which is followed by rain. These storms sometimes last for half an hour or more; and when they disperse they leave the air greatly freshened, and the sky of a deep, clear, and transparent blue. When they occur near the full moon, the whole atmosphere is illuminated by a soft but brilliant silver light, attended with gentle airs, as Shakespeare has expressed—

> "When the sweet wind did gently kiss the trees,
> "And they did make no noise."

Passing by the city of Moorshedabad, on the evening of a Mussulman holiday, I was much entertained to see the river covered with innumerable lights, just floating above the surface of the water. Such an uncommon appearance was, at first, difficult to account for; but I found, upon enquiry, that upon these occasions they fabricate a number of small lamps, which they light and set afloat on the river: the stream constantly running down, they are carried to a

considerable diſtance, and laſt for many hours. After a paſ-
ſage of a few days from Mongheir, I arrived at Calcutta. Several of the ſubjects I had collected in my journey were painted for the Honourable the then Governor General; two of them on a large ſcale, viz. the Falls of Mootejerna, and the Ruins of Rajemahel.

CHAP. III.

Embark in the Train of the Governor General—Boats of the Country deſcribed—Remarks on thoſe of the South Sea—Views on the River—Dutch, French, and Daniſh Settlements—Sir Eyre Coote's—Coſſimbuzen—Sir John D'Oyley's—Patna—Reception of the Governor there—Moſque of Moonhier—Arrive at Buxar—Gazipoor—Curious Ruins—Benares—Arreſt of the Rajah—Inſurrection at Benares—Principal Events of the War—Flight from Benares, and Return thither.

I DID not remain long in the capital of Bengal, on my return from Mongheir, before a new opportunity was preſented to me of again indulging the curioſity which I felt both as an artiſt and a man, to enlarge my acquaintance with a country ſo fertile in the beauties of nature at leaſt. It being determined by the Bengal Government that it was expedient, for the public utility, that the Governor General ſhould make a tour through a part of the country, Mr. Haſtings, with that liberality and attention to the arts which has ever characterized his conduct, acceded to my requeſt, and permitted me to accompany him.

On the 25th of June, 1781, therefore, I embarked in a budgerow for this expedition. The periodical rains had now commenced, and every natural object prefented a new face, with fuch a frefhnefs of verdure, and with fuch vigour and fulnefs of foliage, that all nature appeared in the utmoft luxuriance. From the number of gentlemen who neceffarily attended the Governor General, the fleet was very large, and confifted of every variety of the boats of the country, except thofe which are called burs, and of which we met with feveral in our courfe. Thefe veffels are large rude barks, the fides of which are raifed very high, and fewed together with the fibres of the cocoa nut tree. They have only a fingle maft, with a large fquare fail, and the bottoms of them are nearly flat. They take in a great quantity of water from their fides and bottoms, which compels the crew to employ fome people continually in bailing. They are ufed for the carriage of cotton, and other very bulky materials, the weight of which cannot bear any proportion to their fize. Indeed, it would be impracticable to employ boats which were calculated to draw any confiderable quantity of water on this river, as the navigation is extremely dangerous, from the fands being conftantly fhifting. I have known an ifland, four miles in length, and containing fome villages, wholly fwept away in one feafon; in the mean time, at a little diftance, other iflands were formed, from the fands being thrown up. This phenomenon took place off the point of Rajemahel, in the year 1782.

THE boats uſed by the natives for travelling, and alſo by Europeans, are the budgerows, which both ſail and row: they have in general from twelve to twenty oars. Theſe boats vary in their ſize according to the condition of their owners; ſome may be about ſixty feet in length, having very high ſterns; many of them twelve feet from the water's edge, and quite ſharp at the upper point: in the center they are broad, having a conſiderable bearing in the water, and quite ſharp forward. They are ſteered with a large paddle or oar, extending ten feet from the ſtern; and there is generally one maſt in the center, on which is hoiſted a large ſquare ſail: they have likewiſe a topmaſt, on which is a ſquare ſail for fine weather. Theſe boats are ill calculated to go near the wind, and indeed are dangerous, from the great weight abaft; they are, however, extremely commodious, having in the center a ſmall verander, or open portico, opening by a door into a handſome room, lighted by a range of windows on each ſide. This is the dining or ſitting room, within which is a convenient bed chamber, generally containing a ſmall cloſet: the heighth of the ſitting room is uſually from ſeven to nine feet. Beſides this boat, a gentleman is uſually attended by two others; a pulwah, for the accommodation of the kitchen, and a ſmaller boat, a paunchway, which is deſtined to convey him either on ſhore or on board, as it frequently happens that the budgerow cannot come cloſe to the ſhores, where he might wiſh to land. Theſe boats ſail more expeditiouſly than the budgerows; but the paunchways are nearly of the ſame general conſtruction, with this difference, that the greateſt breadth is ſomewhat farther aft, and the ſterns lower: the pulwahs are a broad boat, and not ſo ſharp forward or aft as the other two. The Engliſh gentlemen have made great improvements on the budgerow in Bengal, by introducing a broad flat floor, ſquare ſterns, and broad bows: Theſe boats are much ſafer, ſail near and keep their wind, and there is no danger attending their taking the ground; they are, beſides, calculated for carrying a greater quantity of ſail. Another boat of this country, which is very curiouſly conſtructed, is called a Moor-punky: theſe are very long and narrow, ſometimes extending to upwards of an hundred feet in length, and not more than eight feet in breadth; they are always paddled, ſometimes by forty men, and are ſteered by a large paddle from the ſtern, which riſes either in the ſhape of a peacock, a ſnake, or ſome other animal. The perſons employed to paddle are directed by a man who ſtands up, and ſometimes he makes uſe of a branch of a plant to direct their motions. In one part of the ſtern is a canopy ſupported by pillars, in which are ſeated the owner and his friends, who partake together of the refreſhing breezes of the evening. Theſe boats are very expenſive, owing to the beautiful decorations of painted and gilt ornaments, which are highly varniſhed, and exhibit a very conſiderable degree of taſte. It was curious to me to obſerve the perfect ſimilarity in manners between the inhabitants of this country and the people of Otaheite in theſe water excursions. The pleasure boats of the South Sea islanders are, in many instances, similar to these: working in an ocean, they found the necessity of applying an out rigger, or of lashing two vessels together, to prevent oversetting. Like the boats I am speaking of, they are worked by paddles, and are also directed by a man holding a branch, who, in common with the person in the Moor-punky, uses much gesticulation, and tells his story to excite either laughter or exertion. My former passage down the river to Calcutta was too rapid to allow of more observation than what related to the general appearance of the villages and towns on its banks. The stream is usually calculated to run at the rate of five miles an hour; but the rapidity of the flood, during the rainy season, is increased, and round some of the points in the river it is very great. Should it be calm weather when the flood is thus impetuous, the boatmen endure much fatigue in towing round these points against the stream, and particularly so where the banks are very high; and some of them, in the great river, are equal to the top of the mast of a common budgerow.

At a small distance above Calcutta is the Danish settlement of Serampoor, where there is a neat town, which carries on a considerable trade. Both sides of the river are decorated with a few houses belonging to English gentlemen: at Ghiretty, twenty miles from Calcutta, is a very fine seat, which, in the year 1781, was inhabited by the family of the late Sir Eyre Coote, who at that time was fighting the battles of his country on the plains of the Carnatic; where his health and life fell a facrifice to his great exertions. With an army of never more than feven thoufand effective men, this experienced General kept the whole power of Hyder Ally at bay, and at all times was fuperior in action to the multitudes of the enemy, who were fupported by a moft formidable train of artillery, and immenfe bodies of cavalry.

A LITTLE above this is the French fettlement of Chandernagore, and the ruins of the fort evince it to have been confiderable. The fort was deftroyed by Commodore Watfon in 1758, in a fevere action, which was particularly diftinguifhed by the gallantry of Captain Speke, who loft his fon on the quarter-deck of his own fhip during the engagement. Near to this is the town of Chinfurah, the Dutch fettlement, on the banks of the river: this town is very diftinguifhable at a confiderable diftance, and has a handfome appearance. It contains feveral good houfes, and a church, with a little mole projecting into the river. Chinfurah lies nearly midway between Chandernagore and the old town of Hoogly, which is now nearly in ruins, but poffeffes many veftiges of its former greatnefs. In the beginning of this century it was the great mart for the export trade of Bengal to Europe. From this place we pafs by Culna and Nuddea, (both confiderable towns) in our way to Cutwa, which was made famous by the retreat of Aliverdy Cawn, in the face of a large Marhatta army, in May 1742. After passing Plassy, which has been already mentioned, is the great military station, in Bengal, Burhampoor, where there are barracks for ten thousand men; and a little above is the island of Cossimbuzar, in which is a factory belonging to the English company, where a commercial resident is constantly stationed: the gentleman then resident was Mr. S. Droz, whose polite attentions to me I shall always remember with pleasure. On this island there is likewise a Dutch factory. At a short distance from Cossimbuzar is the city of Moorshedabad, where, at the period of which I am speaking, resided Sir John D'Oyley, then engaged in a political department. The liberality and attentions of this gentleman to every person travelling this road are well known; and in his house, I may truly say, reigned the very spirit of old English hospitality. From Moorshedabad the Hoogly river continues to Sooty, where is the entrance into the Ganges. From this place to Mongheir it is usual to keep on the western shore, and nearly all the way to Patna, unless a leading breeze from the southward and eastward should enable the boatmen to steer as nearly from point to point as the shoals will admit. Every where on either side of the river there are collections of villages, and the country is in high cultivation.

When the fleet arrived at the city of Patna the shores were lined with people, the windows in the houses on the banks of the river were filled, even the tops of the buildings and every wall was crouded, ſo that when the Governor General went on ſhore, it was ſcarcely poſſible to proceed, from the multitude, which preſſed on every ſide, to ſalute him. When he had paſſed them, all appeared ſtruck with the ſimplicity of his appearance, and his ready and conſtant attention to prevent any injury to the meaneſt individual from the irraſcibility of his Chubdars, or other ſervants, who endeavoured to keep them from preſſing in. They could not but contraſt this appearance and conduct with that of their Nabobs, whom they had never ſeen except mounted on lofty elephants, and glittering in ſplendor with their train, followed by the ſoldiery to keep off the multitude from offending their arrogance and pride.

THE city of Patna, the principal ſeat of the province and government of Bahar, is long and narrow, containing a great number of inhabitants: this is the reſidence of the political and commercial chiefs, and the courts of juſtice of the province. It has been famous for ages. Major Rennel, whoſe judgement is ſcarcely to be diſputed, places the ancient city of Palebothra upon the ſcite of Patna. The buildings are high, and the ſtreets narrow and far from clean. Patna contains a fort, in which were confined the priſoners taken by Meer Coſſim, Nabob of Bengal, in the war of 1764, by whoſe order they were maſſacred. The execution of this moſt atrocious act was committed to Summaroo, a French renegado in the ſervice of the Nabob. The conſequence of this ſcene of horror was, the expulſion of the Nabob, who afterwards drew the late Sujah ul Dowlah, Nabob of Oude, into a war with the Engliſh, which terminated ſo favourably and ſo honourably to the Britiſh character at the battle of Buxar; when a peace was made, leaving the conquerors in the undiſturbed poſſeſſion of Bengal, Bahar, and part of Orixa. Meer Coſſim became afterwards, from his crimes, an outcaſt from ſociety, and is reported to have died of want under the walls of Delhi, being prohibited from entering the city.

FROM Patna I made an excurſion inland, about five coſs, to view the moſque of Moonhier, on the river Soane. This building, though not large, is certainly very beautiful: it is a ſquare, with pavilions riſing from the angles; and in the center is a majeſtic dome, the top of which is finiſhed by what the Indian architects call a cullus: the line of the curve of the dome is not broken, but is continued by an inverted curve until it finiſhes in a creſcent. I cannot but greatly prefer this to the manner in which all great domes are finiſhed in Europe, by erecting a ſmall building on the top, which, at the point of contact with the dome, has a ſharp angle. The outer ſurface of this dome is ornamented by plantane leaves cut in ſtone, covering the whole; the lines interſect each other in great lozenges, and form altogether a beautiful ornament. The great entrance to the moſque is ſimilar to many of the doors to our large Gothic cathedrals, having columns diminiſhing as it were in perſpective to the inner door. There is a large tank belonging to it, with ſeveral buildings riſing from the water, containing pavilions. The whole, however, is much decayed.

THE river Soane falls into the Ganges a little above Patna: at a ſmall diſtance from Patna is Bankepour, where are the reſidences of the Engliſh gentlemen, and near to which is the military ſtation of Dinapour.

FROM Patna I followed the fleet, and paſſed the mouth of the river Caramnaſſa, the boundary of Bahar, and on the 12th of Auguſt arrived at Buxar. This is a fort and ſmall military ſtation, and was, at the time I was there, commanded by Major Eaton. We proceeded from this place to Gazipoor, on the eaſtern ſhore of the Ganges. At this place are the ruins of a fine palace, built in the beginning of this century. It is raiſed on a high bank, and on a point commanding two great reaches of the river, up and down. From the bank, which is full thirty feet from the water, is raiſed another baſement of brick and maſonry fifteen feet high, in which are ſome apartments: on this is the building, which is an oblong ſquare, with great pavilions at the angles, and in the center of each ſide: the whole is an open ſpace, ſupported by colonades ſurrounding it. Within, on the floor of the building, is a channel for water about four feet wide; it encircles the floor, and, at equal ſpaces, there were formerly fountains. In the center of the building is a ſpace ſufficient to contain twenty people.

NEARLY adjoining to this palace is a building for the purpoſe of raiſing water for the fountains, and ſupplying them by the means of pipes, which communicate with each other.

ABOUT two miles inland from the river are the remains of a ſerai; and, nearly adjoining, tombs, built at the ſame period as the palace. Theſe buildings are in a fine taſte of Mooriſh architecture, and in very good repair. Views of both the palace and tombs are exhibited to the public in a work which I publiſhed, containing Views in India.

FROM Gazipoor I proceeded to Benares, a diſtance of twenty Engliſh miles, and arrived there the day after the Governor General with his ſuite.

I FELT a real pleaſure on my arrival at this place, from being able to contemplate the pure Hindoo manners, arts, buildings, and cuſtoms, undepraved by any intermixture with the Mahomedans; and laid my plans for obſerving with the utmoſt attention whatever came within the ſphere of a painter's notice. The unhappy events that immediately ſucceeded fruſtrated, for the preſent, thoſe deſigns.

It would give me pleaſure to ſatisfy the curioſity of the reader concerning the circumſtances of that war, but it would be foreign to the object of theſe pages to enter upon a minute detail; and the public is already in poſſeſſion of the great outline of the facts. Some notes, however, which I made on the ſpot, and at the time, may prove not quite uninteresting, and I flatter myſelf will contain ſomething of original information.

It is not my buſineſs to enter into the queſtion reſpecting the rights of the government in different countries and thoſe of the governed. Facts are my object, and ſuch alone as fell within the limited and confined ſphere of my notice. On my arrival, the 15th of Auguſt, the general converſation turned upon the conduct of Cheyt Sing, the Zemendar of the province. It is neceſſary in this place to remark, that the word Zemendar implies ſimply a land-holder, either by a right of inheritance, or as a renter merely; if by right of inheritance, the government, virtually being the proprietors of the ſoil, if they think proper may poſſeſs themſelves of it by the laws of Hindoſtan, paying to the Zemendar ten per cent. out of ſuch Zemendary. Rajah Cheyt Sing had met the Governor General at Buxar, attended with a conſiderable train, and a large fleet of boats, in which were two thouſand armed men, ſelected from the flower of the military of Benares, and ſuppoſed at the time, and reaſonably ſo, to be intended for the purpoſe of ſupporting him in the refuſal of ſuch demands as might be made upon him by the Governor General, and to prevent the exertion of force in ſupport of the Britiſh authority.

The cauſe of diſagreement between the Britiſh government and the Zemendar of Benares is well known. It is, however, merely an act of common juſtice to ſtate, that, during my whole reſidence in India, I never ſo much as heard the guilt and perfidy of Cheyt Sing once called in queſtion. It was notorious that he was in the intereſt of the enemy; and it was equally notorious that he with-held, under the moſt trifling and falſe pretences, the aſſiſtance which was demanded of him, and which by the nature of his treaty he was bound to furniſh: in a word, it was notorious to every perſon that he wanted only a convenient opportunity to withdraw his allegiance from the company.

After ſeveral letters and meſſages had paſſed between Cheyt Sing and the Governor General, the Reſident, Mr. Markham, received orders to put the Rajah under arreſt, at his houſe at Sewalla Gaut, on the banks of the river, to which he quietly ſubmitted, without any appearance of oppoſition. This was on the 16th; and about one o'clock in the afternoon we were informed that a large body of the Rajah's people had croſſed from Ramnagur to the Benares ſide of the river, and had ſurrounded the Rajah's houſe. A note was at the ſame time received by the Reſident, Mr.

Markham, from Lieutenant Staulker, who had been left with two companies of Major Popham's grenadier ſeapoys as a guard, ſaying that the people began to be troubleſome, and requeſting an immediate ſupply of ammunition. It was now found that ſuch delicacy had been obſerved towards the Rajah, in order to prevent any ſuſpicion being entertained of an intention to carry the puniſhment farther than was really propoſed, that the ſeapoys muſkets were not loaded, nor had they (as no ſerious oppoſition was expected) any ammunition. To this unfortunate circumſtance may be attributed the unhappy fate of three very gallant officers, Lieutenants Staulker, Scott, and Sims, and two compleat companies of grenadier ſeapoys, not more than twenty eſcaping with their lives, and numbers of thoſe miſerably wounded.

As ſoon as the diſturbance became known, Major Popham, who was then at Benares, ſet off immediately for his camp at Marwaddy, about two coſs (or four miles) from the town, to lead the remainder of his people to the aſſiſtance of their fellow ſoldiers. His utmoſt exertions enabled them to arrive only in ſufficient time to be the melancholy ſpectators of this horrid ſlaughter, without the power of revenging it, as the rebels had diſperſed, and the Rajah had found means to make his eſcape.

Fortunately for the Engliſh party in Benares, the rebels were ſatisfied with what they had effected, the liberation of the Rajah and the maſſacre of the ſeapoys; but had they attacked the Governor General in his then defenceleſs ſituation, every perſon with him muſt have fallen a ſacrifice to their fury.

THE following day every Engliſhman attended the funeral of Lieutenants Staulker, Scott, and Sims; and ſome time after a monument to their memory was raiſed over their remains. The gloom that ſucceeded was truly melancholy; the buſineſs of the city was ſtopt, and it was deſerted by great numbers of the inhabitants. In paſſing through the ſtreets knots of people, all of them armed, were obſerved ſecretly conſulting. From this ſituation we were rouſed by an unhappy affair, ariſing from the ill-judged ambition of Captain Mayaffer, who commanded the remainder of Major Popham's detachment at Mizapoor, on the oppoſite ſide of the river, conſiſting of a battalion of ſeapoys, and Captain Doxat's corps of chaſſeurs, reinforced by Captain Blair's battalion of ſeapoys from Chunar. This officer, contrary to poſitive orders, led the troops to the attack of Ramnagur, a fort and town on the oppoſite ſide of the river to Benares. The ſtreets of this town are narrow, and every houſe being built with ſtone, they became each a fortification, which was filled with the Rajah's people. The conſequence of this raſh conduct was, the loſs of Captain Mayaffer, Captain Doxat, thirty-three of the corps of chaſſeurs, two guns, one howitzer, and one hundred and three men of all denominations. The news of this check reached us on the 21ſt. in the morning, and was ſoon followed by advices of the intentions of the rebels to make an attack on Benares that night; it was therefore thought adviſable to leave this place of inſecurity for Chunar, a diſtance of twenty miles. This reſolution was taken at ſeven in the evening, and the whole party was clear of the town by half paſt eight o'clock. The confuſion natural on ſuch an occaſion ſoon ſubſided; and the party, including ſervants, &c. with the troops, which amounted to about four hundred men, ſafely arrived oppoſite Chunar in the morning at ſeven o'clock. The night fortunately turned out the moſt favourable poſſible; it was light, clear, and cool. As the reſolution was ſuddenly taken, I was under the neceſſity of leaving behind me the whole of my baggage, excepting my drawings, and a few changes of linen, which I had thrown into my pallankeen, and which in the confuſion of the night I loſt ſight of, but found my ſervants on the following day. In the party was Beneram Pundit, the Berar Vakeel,* and his brother Biſſumber Pundit, who, from motives of the ſtrongeſt perſonal attachment to Mr. Haſtings, left their family in Benares, to attend him, and ſet what in that country is a very extraordinary example, a native voluntarily ſharing in the dangers and diſtreſſes of a European, without a view to his own private advantage.

* Vakeel is an Agent from one court to another.

On this occafion it cannot be improper to mention the handfome and liberal conduct of every gentleman in the garrifon of Chunar to thofe who attended the Governor General. I feel ftrongly the attentions fhewn me at this time by my friend Major, now Colonel Gardner, at whofe houfe, during my ftay at Chunar, I received every kind of hofpitality.

The war was now completely commenced, with great difadvantage on the part of the Englifh; their number fmall, and befieged in a fort, without provifion to laft a month, or money to pay the few troops, which were already confiderably in arrears, owing to the mifconduct of the Rajah, who had now fixed his ftandard on the fort of Lutteefpoor, in the jungles,* and who was recruiting his army. The feveral orders that had been fent by the Governor General to the commanding officers, who were within a moderate diftance, to march to his affiftance, were either cut off by the enemy, or, from the fears of the meffengers, thefe orders were fecreted, and were never heard of afterwards. One of the Hircarrahs,† however, reached Lieutenant Polhil, then at Allahabad, who immediately marched with his corps of three hundred and eighty men, and reached the oppofite fhore of Chunar on the 27th. In the mean time, a perfon in the fervice of

* Jungles, clofe woods.

† Hircarrahs are fervants, ufed for carrying orders or meffages to any diftance.

Cheyt Sing, at Iionpoor, on the river Goomty, had collected a body of two thouſand matchlock men, and one hundred and fifty horſe, and had taken poſt at a ſmall fort called Seker, on the oppoſite ſide of the river to Chunar. This man Lieutenant Polhil received orders to attack on the following morning, which order he executed with ſucceſs: he drove the enemy, and took poſſeſſion of the fort, and ſecured a conſiderable quantity of grain. This was a valuable acquiſition to the party, for it was now found, from the temper of the people and the complexion of the times, that ſcarcely as much grain could be procured as would ſerve the daily conſumption of the garriſon. The Rajah's force at this time was ſaid to be ten thouſand ſtrong, and his oſtenſible force was daily increaſing.

MAJOR Popham's camp lay at two miles diſtance from the fort; and on the third of September he detached a party, under the command of Captain Blair, with an intention to break up a camp of the enemy which was formed under the walls of Pateeta, and which was carried into execution with great gallantry, though with conſiderable loſs. Pateeta is a large town, ſurrounded by a rampart, and defended by a fort.

THE news of the inſurrection had ſpread to a conſiderable diſtance, and a force was detached from Cawnpoor, and from Lucknow, to the aſſiſtance of the Governor General, under Majors Crab and Roberts, the firſt of which reached Chunar on the 10th of September, and the latter gentleman on the 13th. Effective meaſures were then taken to put a final period to the war, by attacking vigorouſly both the fort of Pateeta and that of Lutteefpoor, and both attacks happily ſucceeded on the ſame day, the Rajah flying from Lutteefpoor to take ſanctuary in his ſtrong hold of Bidjegur. I ſhould have remarked, that Pateeta lies about four miles north of Chunar, and Lutteefpoor ten miles beyond, in the ſame direction: Bidjegur is fifty miles from Chunar.

THE cruel and ſanguinary diſpoſition of Cheyt Sing was manifeſted, during his reſidence in Lutteefpoor, by an action of peculiar atrocity. Some wounded men who were taken priſoners in the camp that was left at Mirzapoor, on the retreat of the troops after the unhappy affair of Captain Mayaffer, had been conveyed to Lutteefpoor, where they were detained as priſoners. Upon hearing of the ſucceſs of Captain Blair's party, the Rajah ordered the unhappy men to be bound and carried into the woods, and to be there maſſacred in cold blood. One poor creature only eſcaped in a very mangled condition into Chunar.

THE fort of Chunar is ſituated on the Ganges, near twenty miles above the city of Benares: it is built on a rock, which is fortified all round by a wall, and towers at various diſtances. At that end overlooking the river is ſituated the citadel, which has formerly been ſtrong. This fort is ſaid to be of the higheſt antiquity, and originally built by the Hindoos. In the citadel there is an altar, conſiſting of a plain black marble ſlab, on which the tutelary deity of the place is traditionally at all times ſuppoſed to be ſeated, except from ſun-riſe until nine o'clock in the morning, when he is at Benares, during which time, from the ſuperſtition of the Hindoos, attacks may be made with a proſpect of ſucceſs. In various parts of the fort there are old ſculptures of the Hindoo divinities, now nearly defaced by time. There are likewiſe on the gates ſome old Perſian inſcriptions, mentioning in whoſe reign, and by whom, the fort was repaired and ſtrengthened.

THIS has always been conſidered as a poſt of great conſequence upon the Ganges, from its inſulated ſituation, projecting forwards to a conſiderable extent, and being of conſiderable heighth. It was beſieged by the Engliſh in the war carried on, during the years 1764 and 1765, againſt the late Nabob Sujah ul Dowlah when he joined Meer Coſſim, and was gallantly defended by its commandant, an Abyſſinian in the ſervice of that prince.

THE firſt attempt of the Engliſh againſt Chunar was unſucceſsful; but afterwards, on the fall of Allahabad, the commandant finding that the whole country had ſubmitted to the Engliſh, and that his maſter's affairs were deſperate, thought it needlefs to hold out any longer, and on the 7th of February, 1765, he furrendered the Fort to Major, now General Stibbert; it was afterwards reftored to the Nabob, when the peace was fettled with that Prince; and in 1772, it was formally ceded by him to the Englifh Eaft India Company, in exchange for the Fort of Allahabad. At this place is kept the magazine of ammunition and artillery for the Brigade at Cawnpore.

During my ftay at Chunar I made feveral drawings of the Fort, and one of Pateeta. As the war was, however, now concluded, except obtaining poffeffion of Bidjegur (to which place Major Popham proceeded with his whole force), the whole party returned with the Governor General, through Ramnagur, to Benares, and arrived there the 28th of September; after which I had fufficient leifure and opportunity for my particular and profeffional purfuits.

CHAP. IV.

Deſcription of Benares—Elegant Faſcade—Hindoo Temples—Diſſertation on the Hindoo, Mooriſh, and Gothic Architecture.

THE city of Benares being the capital of a large diſtrict, and particularly marked as the ſeat of the Bramin learning, it cannot but be conſidered as an object of particular curioſity, more eſpecially, ſince the ſame manners and cuſtoms prevail amongſt theſe people at this day, as at the remoteſt period that can be traced in hiſtory: and in no inſtances of religious or civil life have they admitted of any innovations from foreigners. According to univerſal report, this is one of the moſt ancient Hindoo cities; and if the accounts of their own antiquity may be depended upon, it is, perhaps, the oldeſt in the world. Major Rennell, however, entertains a different opinion on this ſubject, from its not being mentioned by the Syrian Embaſſadors ſoon after the time of Alexander, and from its being unnoticed by Pliny; and I have too great a deference for ſuch an authority, to be at all inclined to diſpute it, whatever may be the claims to antiquity which are preferred in favour of this city.

IT certainly is curious, and highly entertaining to an inquiſitive mind, to aſſociate with a people whoſe manners are more than three thouſand years old; and to obſerve in them that attention and poliſhed behaviour which uſually marks the moſt highly civilized ſtate of ſociety.

The diſtance of Benares from Calcutta, by the neareſt road, according to Major Rennell, is 460 miles; by water, that diſtance is greatly increaſed. This city anciently bore the name of Kaſi, but at what period it received its preſent name the page of hiſtory is ſilent. It is built on the north ſide of the river, which is here very broad, and the banks of which are very high: from the water, its appearance is extremely beautiful; the great variety of the buildings ſtrikes the eye, and the whole view is much improved by innumerable flights of ſtone ſteps, which are either entrances into the ſeveral temples, or to the houſes. Several Hindoo temples greatly embelliſh the banks of the river, and are all aſcended to by Gauts, or flights of ſteps, ſuch as I have already noticed. Many other public and private buildings poſſeſs alſo conſiderable magnificence. Several of theſe I have painted, and ſome on a large ſcale, ſuch as I conceived the ſubjects demanded. Many buildings on the banks of the river, which engage the attention, and invite to further obſervation, prove, on a more minute inveſtigation, to be only embankments, to prevent the overflowing of the water from carrying away the banks at the ſeaſon of the periodical rains, and for ſome time after, when the river is high, and the current ſtrong. The moſt conſiderable of theſe embankments is called Gelſi Gaut; the ſplendor and elegance of which, as a building, I was induced to examine, but found, upon aſcending the large flight of ſteps from the river, nothing behind this beautiful faſcade but the natural bank, and on the top a planted garden. In the centre of the building, over the river, is a kind of turret, raiſed and covered, for the purpoſe of enjoying the freſhneſs of the evening air; and, at the extreme angles, two pavilions crowned with domes, which have the ſame deſtination. Moſt of theſe buildings have been erected by the charitable contributions of the wealthy, for the benefit of the public.

Nearly in the centre of the city is a conſiderable Mahomedan moſque, with two minarets: the height from the water to the top of the minarets is 232 feet. This building was raiſed by that moſt intolerant and ambitious of human beings, the Emperor Aurungzebe, who deſtroyed a magnificent temple of the Hindoos on this ſpot, and built the preſent moſque, of the ſame extent and height as the building he deſtroyed.

The ſtreets in the city are narrow, and not kept in ſuch good order as I expected, from ſome Hindoo villages I had before ſeen. The houſes are very high; I obſerved ſome in which I counted five ſtories, each inhabited by different families. The more wealthy Hindoos, however, live in detached houſes, with open courts, ſurrounded by a wall. The heat, in this place, is conſidered as very great in the hot months, not only from its natural ſituation, but from the houſes being all built of free ſtone, as well as from the narrowneſs of the ſtreets, which produce double and treble reflections of the ſun's rays: from the month of March, therefore, to the uſual ſetting in of the rains in the latter end of June, its heat muſt be intolerable.

Surrounding the city are many ruins of buildings, the effects of Mahomedan intolerance. One is a large circular edifice, having evidently been a Hindoo temple, or part of one; there are ſtill veſtiges of ſome of the ornaments; and on one part I found the Grecian ſcroll.

During my ſtudies at Benares, when I was making drawings of ſome Bramins, and ſeveral other perſons who were entering and departing from a temple named Viſs Viſsha, my attention was called to the building itſelf, and the more I regarded it, the more I was ſurprized to diſcover ornaments upon it which were familiar to my eyes. I then determined to make a ſketch of the whole, which I executed, as well as a more complete drawing of one of the columns; for on accurately obſerving the building in all its parts, I found each column to contain the different ornaments which were found in the other parts of the building.

A COLUMN taken from the TEMPLE of VIS VISHA at BENARES.

Engraved by T. Medland from a Drawing made on the Spot by W. Hodges R.A.

London, Published by J. Edwards, Pall Mall, Jan.y 1. 1793.

For the ſatisfaction of my readers a very careful engraving is annexed, which was executed from the drawing made upon the ſpot.

It is certainly curious to obſerve moſt of the ornamental parts of Grecian architecture appearing in a building erected on the plains of Hindoſtan. I was indeed much ſtruck with this circumſtance, and led to reflect upon it ſo frequently, that I was at length tempted to commit to paper a few thoughts on theſe different ſtyles of architecture, which, in the form of a pamphlet upon the ſubject, was accompanied by two large plates engraved from pictures, entitled, *Views of the Gate leading to the Tomb of Acbar at Secundii, and the Mauſoleum of the Emperor Shere Shah at Saſſeram.* As the eſſay accompanying theſe plates was printed on a ſcale equal to the plates, and as I have ſince found that it could not on that account be read with any convenience, I determined to introduce the ſubſtance of it in this place, as being immediately connected with the ſubject which is now before us, and I conceive perfectly calculated for a work profeſſedly dedicated, in ſome meaſure, to the hiſtory and progreſs of the arts in India.

As I am neither ſufficiently qualified, nor willing to loſe myſelf in the unfathomable, and perhaps impenetrable darkneſs of Eaſtern antiquities, I ſhall not, for the preſent, ſay any thing on the characteriſtic difference of the original Hindoo, and the more modern ſtyle of Mooriſh Architecture, in which all the great monuments are conſtructed; but I ſhall confine myſelf to a few looſe remarks on the prototypes, or firſt models of architecture, as far as it is an art both of taſte and convenience.

THAT the Grecian Architecture comprizes all that is excellent in the art, I cannot help conſidering as a doctrine, which is in itſelf as erroneous and ſervile, as in its conſequences it is deſtructive of every hope of improvement. Architecture undoubtedly ſhould, and muſt be adapted, to all the climates and countries which mankind inhabit, and is variouſly, more than any other art, influenced and modified by the nature of the climate and materials, as well as by the habits and purſuits of the inhabitants.

I HAVE not read Father Ladola's famous diſſertation on the abſurdity of the miſplaced and unprincipled imitation of Greek architecture; nor am I in the leaſt prejudiced againſt its very eminent beauties and perfections: but why ſhould we admire it in an excluſive manner; or, blind to the majeſty, boldneſs, and magnificence of the Egyptian, Hindoo, Mooriſh, and Gothic, as admirable wonders of architecture, unmercifully blame and deſpiſe them, becauſe they are more various in their forms, and not reducible to the preciſe rules of the Greek hut, prototype, and column? or becauſe in ſmaller parts, perhaps accidentally ſimilar, their proportions are different from thoſe to which we are become familiar by habit.

Allowing what muſt be allowed, that the Greek columns, as they are drawn and applied by genius, are the moſt beautiful ſtone repreſentations of the wooden props or ſupports of their original hut, and that in their general forms, and each ſubordinate part, they are the *ne plus ultra* of ſimplicity, ſtrength, and elegance, ſhall we precipitately determine, that the whole excellence of architecture depends on the column alone, or forget that its great effect depends rather upon the great maſſes and forms, and upon the ſymmetry, ſtrength, and conveniency?

However partial I muſt feel, from habit and education, to the Greeks, whoſe free and unfettered genius, in a long ſeries of ages, improved the original hut of a woody country into the incomparable beauties of a marble temple or palace; yet I freely avow that this by no means prevents my entertaining a ſimilar partiality for countries, where different models have been brought to an equal perfection. The forms of the firſt habitations have differed, as the reſpective countries, climates, and manners of the builders, and as the nature, abundance, or ſcantineſs of materials have directed.

Caverns, deep vallies, ſhaggy over-hanging rocks, hollow trees, and the thick impenetrable foliage of the foreſt, have been equally the natural retreat and occaſional habitation of the wild beaſts, and of men whom different accidents have left unacquainted with the comforts of ſociety, expoſed to the inclemencies of the ſeaſons, or to the apprehenſion of dangers from animals of prey, or the no leſs dangerous enemies of their own ſpecies. Men are neither born with tools to build with, nor can be ſuppoſed to have intuitively an innate idea of any particular form of habitation, ſuch as bountiful nature has aſſigned to the beaver, the ſwallow, or the bee; but man is born with a native ſenſe of his wants, and with judgment and intellectual powers to improve his ſituation by ſuch means, as the country affords, and as the climate will ſuggeſt.

Thus far I can venture to ſtate, not only from what I have read, but likewiſe by a ſtronger conviction, from what I have ſeen in the various climates and parts of the world in which I have beheld mankind, in almoſt every ſtage of negative or poſitive civilization.

The hollow tree, and the thick foliage of the foreſt, into which even Kings of Ithaca and Britain have retired, are fitter for occaſional than for permanent reſidence. They appear evidently imitated in the wigwams of the torpid, wretched, unſettled Pecherais on the frozen coaſt of Terra del Fuego; of the equally independent, but not more fortunate New Hollanders, in a milder climate; and of the more civilized and ſagacious hunting ſavages of North America.

These wigwams, nearly the ſame every where as to form, differ in various countries only in the nature of the materials they are built with, ſuch as the boughs of trees, ſhrubs, creeping plants, reeds, ſods, and graſs. Now, if any of theſe wandering families of hunters and fiſhermen ſhould become ſtationary, or form into larger ſocieties, they would ſoon be diſpoſed to give to their habitations as much durability and conveniency as their climates, materials, and manner of life would admit of; nor is it probable they would loſe ſight of their prototype, the wigwam, or materially deviate from it in the external form of their more capacious erection. For conſtant reſidence, theſe would be improved into the various thatches and huts which I have ſeen in the South Sea Iſlands, and which the Negroes on the Coaſt of Guinea, and the Hottentots, inhabit; high and low, circular or ſquare, open at all ſides, incloſed with paliſades, matting, or wicker-work hurdles, lattice, or mud walls. They will raiſe them on piles above the ground, and, as it were, ſuſpend them in the air, in countries where the dampneſs of the ſoil, or ſudden inundations, would endanger their lives and property; as on the banks of the Marannon, or Oroonoko, in Guiana, and in the inland parts of Surinam: they will keep them low, and, as it were, ſink them under ground, in cold climates, where heavy blaſts of wind and ſnow teach them ſuch methods of ſelf-defence. Wandering nations, of herdſmen, fiſhermen, and warriors, ſuch as the Arabs, Calmucks, Monguls, Tonqueſees, Tartars, Eſquimeaux, Greenlanders, Laplanders, Samojedes, and Oſtiacks, find in the ſkins of their cattle, of their flocks, and of their fiſhes, materials; and in their camels, horſes, bullocks, and fiſhing boats, conveyances of portable huts, and imitations of their original wigwams, huts and tents, which in ſhape will differ more or leſs, according to the different materials they are made of. We find them of ſeal and rein deer ſkins in the north, of hides, felt, or matting; in Arabia or Tartary, in the form of cones, with ſquare roofs, and open or ſhut at the ſides.

The different habitations will retain more or leſs of their primitive form in proportion as the different builders remain independent and unmixed, unconnected, and in the ſame ſtate and culture; and as habit reconciles the human mind to almoſt every thing, each of theſe nations or tribes will regard their primitive habitations with the ſame eye of partiality as they are prejudiced in favour of their reſpective countries; but when encreaſing opulence, ambition, or ſucceſsful oppreſſion, create artificial wants, and the great look for more convenience and diſtinction, the national primitive hut or tent will be enlarged, and embelliſhed with what is coſtly among them. When emigrations to foreign countries take place, their prototype will follow the coloniſt, and genius will at laſt ſtretch and improve it to the laſt degree of perfection of which it is capable. What this is, or may be, in architecture, we ſee with admiration exemplified in the old Greek and Roman architecture, which is the thatched wooden hut, metamorphosed by genius into a marble edifice, and yet expressing its original parts in such proportions as are consistent with the nature of stone and marble. Agreeably to the same principle, the most elegant Chinese buildings are evidently imitations of the tent made of bamboo, where strength and slender tapering form admit of higher proportions and wider intercolumniations, and must, of course, make the Greek marble column and its narrow intercolumniation appear heavy in comparison with the Chinese. The Chinese idea of the beauties of their architecture must differ from that of the Greeks, and the Greek rule of architectural beauty cannot reasonably be applied to the principle and materials of Chinese buildings. How far all the above prototypes of buildings are improveable, must be left to the future exertions of genius.

The oblong and tapering huts of the people of Easter Island in the Southern Ocean, are hardly improveable in that country, which is almost destitute of timber. An active people, such as its former inhabitants seem to have been, might, indeed, imitate them in stone; but would these huts suggest any idea but that of ribbed oblong arches, tapering on every side? Even the simple wigwam will, under the influence of fortunate circumstances, be adorned by genius with all the pomp of Flora; the rose, the vine, the honey-suckle, and the gourd, will be entwined; they will be formed into cool and shady bowers, like those which the glowing imagination of Milton assigned to our first parents in the Garden of Eden.

The cavern and grotto, by nature fitted for the ſafe retreat and habitation of man, has in itſelf many advantages; in particular, a ſolidity and durability, which art has never been able ſucceſsfully to imitate: its impenetrable ſides and external form are the mountain itſelf.

When airy, ſpacious, and lofty within, on a riſing ground, commanding an extenſive proſpect and a ſpring, on the banks of rivers, or in the cliffs on the ſea ſhore, how deſirable in a burning climate; impenetrable to wind and weather, how acceptable in cold climates, which are deprived of timber. Let us have a nearer view of its gloomy receſſes.

They are indiſcriminately found in every climate; but in mountainous countries only, in which, as the Swiſs philoſophers tell us, with a particular complacency to themſelves, ſagacity ſooner ripens into genius, and in which the materials for building artificial mountains and caves are obvious at every ſtep. Violence and ſuperior force would ſoon take poſſeſſion of thoſe which are fitteſt for habitation and ſafety. The bones and remains of the largeſt and fierceſt wild beaſts, ſuch as the elephant, rhinoceros, lion, tiger, bear, and wolf, formerly the lords of the wilderneſs, are ſtill found in many of them, and conſtitute ſo many proofs of their excluſive poſſeſſion. Is it to be wondered at, that the ſtouteſt, fierceſt, and craftieſt, amongſt the lords of the whole creation, ſhould alſo have laid hold and kept ſimilar poſſeſſion of them from the remoteſt antiquity?

A GOOD cavern was then a ſuperb palace; under certain circumſtances it is ſo ſtill. If theſe great men, or uſurpers, became afterwards objects of ſuperſtitious adoration, or if they have themſelves been the framers of any ſyſtem of ſuperſtition, then we ſhall no longer be at a loſs to account for the almoſt univerſal tradition which characteriſes rocks and caverns as the haunts and ſacred habitations of the Gods; and in conſequence of which the form and gloom of ſuch caverns have been univerſally imitated in the oldeſt temples. Their external form and appearance is the ſpiry rock, the towering cliff, and the mountain in its immenſe extent: How various! how grand! Their inner form, their breaks, and maſſes, how infinitely more various, grand, and majeſtic, than any thing which the poor wigwam, and its moſt ingenious imitations, can ſuggeſt or boaſt of, which, compared to them, dwindle into nothing; their wonderful variety, their ſhape, their ſtructure, combination of parts, and natural ornaments, depend partly on the difference of the cauſes and circumſtances under which they have been formed, and on the nature of the mountains in which they are found. The Granite, which forms the higheſt maſſes of the oldeſt mountains, affects particular forms, and diſplays a mixture of parts, which are either not found, or are leſs diſcernible in other rocks, ſuch as glittering or gold-coloured mica, chryſtal, and a more or leſs hardened baſis, in which theſe are wrapped up and confined. It is found, evidently ſtratified, in uncouth beds of immenſe extent, variouſly inclined, which furniſhes ſolid maſſes of almoſt every ſize and dimenſion.

THE largeſt obeliſks of Egypt have been hewn out of them. When ſhattered or broken by the irreſiſtible ſhock of earthquakes, the impetuoſity of torrents, when worn by the current of rivers, or corroded or mouldered by the ſlower action of froſt, wind, and weather, the horrid cruſh and downfall of mountains preſents the granite blocks and ſtrata in their rude unwieldy immenſity, wildly piled upon each other, ſo as to form, accidentally, huts and caverns beneath. In the ſame manner, they appear naked and laid bare on the weather-beaten tops and prominences of the higheſt mountains.

THE fiſſures and diviſions of the maſſes appear in various directions, agreeably to the force which has acted upon them; and in ſome caſes they are wonderfully equipoiſed and balanced upon each other.

I HAVE been informed by an ingenious and learned friend of mine, well acquainted with the natural hiſtory of Cornwall, that we need not go to Upper Egypt or the Alps for the ſtudy of granite mountains; the whole ſouth-weſterly end of this iſland, beginning at Dartmoor in Devonſhire, and extending through the whole county of Cornwall, to the remoteſt cliffs and rocks of the Scilly Iſlands, is more or lefs a mafs of granite, almoft every where interfected by metallic veins; that this chiefly appears in St. Michael's Mount, in Mount's Bay, on the fouth coaft; that fome metallic veins or lodes, in the high towering cliffs on the north coaft, corroded and decompofed by the furious battering of the fea, have left ftupendous caverns and excavations, of which he mentions one in Wicka Cove, between St. Ives and St. Juft, as particularly grand, and worthy the infpection of the artift, as well as of the natural hiftorian.

In calcareous, moftly ftratified mountains, caverns are more various and common: befides the accidental caves produced by the giving way and tumbling down of mountainous maffes, and the decompofition of metallic and other lodes, more extenfive and fingular excavations are found in them, evidently produced by earthquakes, or by the decompofition of parts of the rocky maffes, or of the ftratified rock falt, which they furrounded and covered. Such are, I am informed, among many others, the caverns near Chudleigh and Plymouth, in Devonfhire, and thofe which are fo juftly famous near Caftleton and Buxton, in Derbyfhire. In thefe laft we behold the undeniable prototype of the lofty femicircular dome, and of the arched vault, of which the hut of the Grecians could not fuggeft the idea. I defcribe them, from the accurate obfervations of the above mentioned ingenious gentleman, as wonderfully regular, and as large conical excavations in the roof of thefe caverns, which examined by the light of torches appeared to resemble so many semicircular or parabolical cupolas, or, to use a less dignified comparison, so many immense bells. The caverns in calcareous, or more modern adventitious mountains, shew in their walls, besides the texture and stratification, petrified marine, or other bodies, which are never found in granite or similar silicious stones; a wonderful variety of glittering spar crystals; and, in particular, incrustations of snow-white spar or stalactite, which either form undulated hangings on their sides, or icicles dripping from their roofs in the shape of columns, pillars, &c. These are the peculiar glories and features of the grotto of Antiparos. I pass over the caverns in slate and the looser grit-stone, to dwell one instant longer on those which are produced by volcanic eruptions, and chiefly by the contraction of cooling lavas. They totally differ in form and features from the preceding: the forms which these assume will resemble the apertures and bubbles which are found in other scoria. Some of them which are found in Iceland will hold numerous flocks of sheep; they are spread hundreds of fathoms in various branches under ground, and have served formerly as strong holds and habitations to the rustic heroes and warriors, whose names are highly celebrated in the traditional history and songs of that country. Fingal's famous and magnificent grotto is a large stratum of columnar basaltes, in the isle of Staffa, though probably it never was fit for habitation, and still less what some philosophers have supposed it to be, the prototype of the column. That caverns in the loofer chalk, grit-ftone, and beds of hardened volcanic afhes, or tufa, are exceedingly improveable; and that caverns have been inhabited and varioufly improved, is, I think, undeniably evident, from what we fee and read in the monuments and antiquities of every part of the world, and particularly from the immenfe excavated works in the ifland of Salfett, on the coaft of Malabar, and many others.

THE eafy tafk of fpecific hiftorical proof I muft leave to others; and requeft my readers juft to confider, that when enlarged and improved natural caverns in rocks and mountains became infufficient to the increafing numbers of men and families, their improvement and enlargement, whatever it might have been, muft naturally bring on imitations of their forms, by artificial excavations of rocks, or artificial grottos, caverns, and catacombs, by the piling up of loofe and moveable natural ftones; and, laftly, by the compofition of brick, or other artificial imitations of natural ftones, which of courfe would produce walls, huts, and houfes of ftone, mud, or brick, and nearly of the fame form.

ONE natural inference may and ought to be drawn from what has been faid, that the feveral fpecies of ftone buildings, which have been brought more or lefs to perfection, (I mean the Egyptian, Hindoo, Moorifh, and Gothic architecture) inftead of being copies of each other, are actually and effentially the fame; the fpontaneous produce of genius in different countries; the neceffary effects of fimilar neceffity and materials; older and younger brothers and ſiſters of the ſame family, conceived, brought up, and bred to more or leſs grandeur, elegance and perfection, in the Egyptian, Hindoo, and other artificial grottos and caverns. The pyramid, the obeliſk, the ſpire ſteeple and minaret, are evidently bold, ſtupendous imitations of the romantic forms of ſpiry, towering rocks, which the imitators of humble huts never preſumed to attempt. The flat roof hundred pillared Egyptian temple, the Indian pagoda, and choultry, are as evident copies of the numerous caverns, cool grottos, and excavations in the rocky banks of the Nile in Upper Egypt, and in the iſland of Elephanta and Salſet near Bombay. Gloom and darkneſs are common and deſirable to both; for Fancy works beſt when involved in the veil of obſcurity. The arched vault and lofty dome was not ſuggeſted to the Egyptians and oldeſt Hindoos by the grotto and ſacred caverns in granite mountains; they are the natural forms of other caverns, and in particular the boaſt, the ſtrength, and glory of more modern Mooriſh and Gothic temples. If the ſingle or grouped pillars, in many of the props and ſupports of artificial caverns, ſhould appear heavy, they muſt be regarded as having been originally props to mountains; and ſuch would be retained in common uſe, till experience found out eaſier and more pleaſing proportions; and till aſpiring genius, at the ſight of airy and lofty caverns, dared to give them lightneſs, and all the fanciful forms and graces of the Gothic ſtyle.

Such are my ſentiments on the origin of theſe different modes of architecture. The Grecian confeſſedly was ſuggeſted by the primitive form of a rural hut in a champaign woody country; and the Oriental and Gothic I conceive has derived its form and its ornaments from thoſe ſurprizing excavations which are found in rocky and mountainous regions. In India theſe heterogeneous ſpecies of building are ſeldom found combined; and I mention the inſtance which gave riſe to this diſcuſſion as very ſingular indeed. By what means this unnatural union has taken place it is impoſſible to determine; and conjecture would only lead us aſtray from the object of theſe pages, which is a narrative and deſcription of facts.

CHAP. V.

Ceremony of Widows devoting themſelves on the Funeral Pile of their Huſbands—Minute Deſcription of the Performance of that horrid Sacrifice—Journey to Bidjegur—Deſcription of the Fort, &c.—Arrival at Bauglepoor—The Author accompanies Mr. Cleveland through a Part of his Diſtrict—Excellent Conduct of Mr. Cleveland in civilizing the Mountaineers—Curious Sacrifice.

WHILE I was purſuing my profeſſional labours in Benares, I received information of a ceremony which was to take place on the banks of the river, and which greatly excited my curioſity. I had often read and repeatedly heard of that moſt horrid cuſtom amongſt, perhaps, the moſt mild and gentle of the human race, the Hindoos; the ſacrifice of the wife on the death of the huſband, and that by a means from which nature ſeems to ſhrink with the utmoſt abhorrence, by burning. Many inſtances of this practice have been given by travellers; thoſe whom I have met with only mention it as taking place among the higheſt claſſes of ſociety, whoſe vanity united with ſuperſtitious prejudices might have dictated the circumſtance; and I confeſs I could not entertain any other ideas, when I obſerved the theatrical parade that ſeemed to attend it. Mr. Holwell, in his curious work entitled Hiſtorical Events relative to India, thus accounts for this more than inhuman practice: "At the demiſe of the mortal part of the Hindoo great law-giver and prophet, Bramah, his wives, inconſolable for his loſs, reſolved not to ſurvive him, and offered themſelves voluntary victims on his funeral pile. The wives of the chief Rajahs, the firſt officers of the ſtate, being unwilling to have it thought that they were deficient in fidelity and affection, followed the heroic example ſet them by the wives of Bramah. The Bramins, a tribe then newly eſtabliſhed by their great legiſlator, pronounced and declared, that the ſpirits of thoſe heroines immediately ceaſed from their tranſmigrations, and had entered the firſt boboon of purification: it followed, that their wives claimed a right of making the ſame ſacrifice of their mortal forms to God, and the manes of their deceaſed huſbands. The wives of every Hindoo caught the enthuſiaſtic (now pious) flame. Thus the heroic acts of a few women brought about a general cuſtom. The Bramins had given it the ſtamp of religion, and inſtituted the forms and ceremonials that were to accompany the ſacrifice, ſubject to reſtriction, which leave it a voluntary act of glory, piety, and fortitude." The author proceeds to ſtate expreſsly, that he has been preſent at many of theſe ſacrifices, and particularly and minutely records one that happened on the 4th of February, 1742-3, near to Coſſimbuzar, of a young widow between ſeventeen and eighteen years of age, leaving at ſo early an age three children, two boys and a girl; the eldeſt he mentions as not then being four years of age. This infatuated heroine was ſtrongly urged to live, for the future care of her infants; but notwithſtanding this, though the agonies of death were painted to her in the ſtrongeſt and moſt lively terms, ſhe, with a calm and reſolved countenance, put her finger into the fire, and held it there a conſiderable time; ſhe then with one hand put fire in the palm of the other, ſprinkled incenſe on it, and fumigated the Bramins. She was then given to underſtand, by ſome of her friends, that ſhe would not be permitted to burn herſelf, and this intimation appeared to give her deep affliction for a few moments; after which ſhe reſolutely replied, that death was in her own power, and that if ſhe was not allowed to burn, according to the principles of her caſt, ſhe would ſtarve herſelf. Her friends, finding her thus peremptory, were obliged at laſt to conſent to the dreadful ſacrifice of this lady, who was of high rank.

The perſon whom I ſaw was of the Bhyſe (merchant) tribe or caſt; a claſs of people we ſhould naturally ſuppoſe exempt from the high and impetuous pride of rank, and in whom the natural deſire to preſerve life ſhould in general predominate, undiverted from its proper courſe by a proſpect of poſthumous fame. I may add, that theſe motives are greatly ſtrengthened by the exemption of this claſs from that infamy with which the refuſal is inevitably branded in their ſuperiors. Upon my repairing to the ſpot, on the banks of the river, where the ceremony was to take place, I found the body of the man on a bier, and covered with linen, already brought down and laid at the edge of the river. At this time, about ten in the morning, only a few people were aſſembled, who appeared deſtitute of feeling at the cataſtrophe that was to take place; I may even ſay that they diſplayed the moſt perfect apathy and indifference. After waiting a conſiderable time the wife appeared, attended by the Bramins, and muſic, with ſome few relations. The proceſſion was ſlow and ſolemn; the victim moved with a ſteady and firm ſtep; and, apparently with a perfect compoſure of countenance, approached cloſe to the body of her huſband, where for ſome time they halted. She then addreſſed thoſe who were near her with compoſure, and without the leaſt trepidation of voice or change of countenance. She held in her left hand a cocoa nut, in which was a red colour mixed up, and dipping in it the fore-finger of her right hand ſhe marked thoſe near her, to whom ſhe wiſhed to ſhew the laſt act of attention. As at this time I ſtood cloſe to her, ſhe obſerved me attentively, and with the colour marked me on the forehead. She might be about twenty-four or five years of age, a time of life when the bloom of beauty has generally fled the cheek in India; but ſtill ſhe preſerved a ſufficient ſhare to prove that ſhe muſt have been handſome: her figure was ſmall, but elegantly turned; and the form of her hands and arms was particularly beautiful. Her dreſs was a looſe robe of white flowing drapery, that extended from her head to the feet. The place of ſacrifice was higher up on the bank of the river, a hundred yards or more from the ſpot where we now ſtood. The pile was compoſed of dried branches, leaves, and ruſhes, with a door on one ſide, and arched and covered on the top: by the ſide of the door ſtood a man with a lighted brand. From the time the woman appeared to the taking up of the body to convey it into the pile, might occupy a ſpace of half an hour, which was employed in prayer with the Bramins, in attentions to thoſe who ſtood near her, and converſation with her relations. When the body was taken up ſhe followed cloſe to it, attended by the chief Bramin; and when it was depoſited in the pile, ſhe bowed to all around her, and entered without ſpeaking. The moment ſhe entered, the door was cloſed; the fire was put to the combuſtibles, which inſtantly flamed, and immenſe quantities of dried wood and other matters were thrown upon it. This laſt part of the ceremony was accompanied with the ſhouts of the multitude, who now became numerous, and the whole ſeemed a maſs of confuſed rejoicing. For my part I felt myſelf actuated by very different ſentiments: the event that I had been witneſs to was ſuch, that the minuteſt circumſtance attending it could not be eraſed from my memory; and when the melancholy which had overwhelmed me was ſomewhat abated, I made a drawing of the ſubject, and from a picture ſince painted the annexed plate was engraved.

In other parts of India, as the Carnatic, this dreadful cuſtom is accompanied in the execution of it with ſtill greater horror. It is aſſerted, that they dig a pit, in which is depoſited a large quantity of combuſtible matter, which is ſet on fire, and the body being let down, the victim throws herſelf into the flaming maſs. In other places, a pile is raiſed extremely high, and the body with the wife is placed upon it, and then the whole is ſet on fire. Whatever is the means, reaſon and nature ſo revolt at the idea, that, were it not a well known and well authenticated circumſtance, it would hardly obtain credit. In truth, I cannot but confeſs, that ſome degree of incredulity was mingled with curioſity on this occaſion; and the deſire of aſcertaining ſo extraordinary a fact was my greateſt inducement to be a ſpectator.

The war which had commenced in this province in Auguſt was not compleatly finiſhed by the month of October, although the Rajah had left the country, and joined the army of the Mahrattas under Madajee Scindia. The ſtrong fortreſs of Bidjegur yet held out againſt the troops commanded by Major Popham; and I was happy to receive the commands of Mr. Haſtings to proceed to Bidjegur to make drawings of that, and of the fort of Lutteefpoor on the road.

After paſſing the open country, (the cultivation of which had ſuffered but in a ſmall degree from the recent

PROCESSION of a HINDOO WOMAN to the Funeral Pile of her HUSBAND.

Engraved by W. Skelton, from a Picture painted by W. Hodges, R.A.

London. Published by J. Edwards, Pall Mall, Jan. 1 1793.

diſturbances) the traveller enters the jungles or woods, which ſurround the fort of Lutteeſpoor. The woods are chiefly compoſed of Bamboos, which come cloſe to the walls of the fort, and are ſo very thick as in ſome parts to be impenetrable. The fort is built of ſtone, with the walls flanked with round towers, and is in a ruinous ſtate. Two miles from the fort is a high and difficult rocky paſs, at the top of which the country continues level and flat, until nearly within three or four miles of Bidjegur, when it ſinks, and there appears a natural foſſe ſurrounding the extremity of the mountain, and the view is terminated in a low ſwampy country, which, in the time of the rains, is overflowed. Between Lutteeſpoor and Bidjegur are conſiderable woods, intermixed with cultivated ground, and a few villages. Bidjegur is fifty miles from Benares, and the fort is ſeated on the top of a high mountain, covered from its baſe to its ſummit with wood. This is the laſt of a long range of mountains, which, at this place, rudely decline to the plain. Here I enjoyed an opportunity which falls to the lot of but few profeſſional men in my line; I mean that of obſerving the military operations of a ſiege. The camp was formed nearly four miles from the fort: there was, however, a rock about the heighth of the top of the mountains, and within gun ſhot, commanding one face of the fort, which was ſquare. From this ſtation the walls were battered; and, after a practicable breach was made, the garriſon thought fit to ſurrender. In the garriſon were found the mother and other female relatives of

Cheyt Sing, to whom every delicate attention was paid. A View of Bidjegur, taken on the ſpot, is ſubjoined.

Soon after Bidjegur was taken, preparations were made for the departure of the party attending the Governor General; and towards the end of December we ſailed, and arrived at Bauglepoor early in January, 1782. As at this place it was my intention to remain for ſome time, I took my leave for the preſent of the gentlemen attending the Governor General, who, in the ſpace of two months out of the ſix ſince we had left Calcutta, had been witneſs to a revolt that had nearly ſhaken the Britiſh power in India to its baſe; but, by the vigorous exertions of the officers, ſeconded by the courage and perſeverance of the troops, under a well regulated plan for the recovery of the power of the Eaſt India Company, every thing terminated in a manner that ſerved to impreſs the powers then at war with the Engliſh with the moſt formidable opinion of the vigour and energy of the Britiſh government. The conduct and gallantry of both officers and troops, in the hour of their utmoſt diſtreſs, were not improbably a means of facilitating the permanent peace with the Mahratta powers, and particularly with Madajee Scindia, which immediately followed.

Soon after the departure of the gentlemen, about the end of January, Mr. Cleveland propoſed to me to accompany him through a part of the diſtrict into the hills, to

A VIEW of BIDJEGUR.

Engraved by B. T. Pouncy from a Picture Painted by W. Hodges R.A. in the Collection of Warren Hastings Esq.re

London, Published by J. Edwards, Pall Mall Jan.y 1.1793.

which I readily acceded; and early in February we ſet out on a tour through a part of the country called the Jungle Terry, to the weſtward of Bauglepoor. This interior part of the country conſiſts of much wood, intermixed with cultivated ground, and many villages, chiefly inhabited by huſbandmen. Among others, I could not but notice the village of Barkope, adjacent to which are many hills, riſing almoſt to the conſequence of mountains, and every one of them is inſulated by the plain country. The appearance of this part of the country is very ſingular, having immenſe maſſes of ſtone piled one on another; from the interſtices of which are very large timber trees growing out, in ſome places overſhadowing the whole of the rocks: the trees are of various kinds. In many of theſe rocks I found the teek, a timber remarkable for its hardneſs and ſize; and this accompanied with the mango, no leſs remarkable for its ſoftneſs, and which produces the fine fruit of that name. The tamarind and other trees are alſo produced here. On ſome of the higheſt of theſe hills I obſerved durgaws, or burial places, with little chapels annexed, belonging to the Muſſulmans.

In the courſe of our journey Mr. Cleveland received an invitation from ſome principal hill chiefs, to the ceremony of an annual ſacrifice, which he accepted; and after the buſineſs was executed which brought him into this part of his diſtrict, we proceeded to the village on the mountain where the ceremony was to take place. The people from whom Mr. Cleveland had received the invitation reſide in a range of hills which lie to the ſouth and to the weſtward of Bauglepoor, extending ſouth to the back of Rajemahel. It has been conjectured by ſome (how well founded I know not) that this people are the aboriginal natives of the country. They have manners certainly different from the Hindoos, being neither divided into caſts nor tribes, and eating of every ſpecies of proviſion which the followers of Bramah cannot, as they are limited in this article according to their caſt. As it is extremely difficult to decide on the claims of different tribes to antiquity, I could not help ſuſpecting that theſe may have been formerly no other than the outcaſts from the Hindoos, who forming themſelves into a ſociety in the receſſes of the country, and poſting themſelves in the more mountainous parts, to prevent being ſurprized, occaſionally iſſued to commit depredations on the defenceleſs people in the plains. On this account, indeed, they became ſo formidable, that the Hindoo, Mooriſh, and afterwards the Engliſh governments, have at all times been under the neceſſity of ſtationing troops, to check their inroads. Like thoſe of all other ſavages, their incurſions have been merely predatory, and what they ſeize is by ſurprize. They generally entered the villages at night, and, murdering the huſbandmen, drove off the cattle, and then ſecured themſelves in their fortreſſes in the hills. As they were only armed with bows and arrows and a ſabre, they were unable either to attack or to withſtand regular troops with fire arms. By lying in wait like a tyger in the woods, they frequently cut off the traveller or ſtragglers, and from parties which had been ſent to chaſtiſe them—nor could they, at any time, be induced to reform from their horrid practices, by the moſt vigorous exertions of the military againſt them, until the time Mr. Cleveland was placed at the head of the diſtrict, whoſe judgment ſuggeſted a plan, which a ſhort time afterwards was carried into effect with the happieſt ſucceſs.

It was the humanity of that gentleman, added to the deſire of improving the revenue of this part of his diſtrict for the Company's benefit, that induced him to venture into the hills, alone and unarmed, where he convened ſome of the principal Chiefs; and after the fulleſt aſſurance of his moſt peaceable intentions and good-will towards them, he invited them to viſit him at his reſidence at Bauglepoor. The confidence which he manifeſted in their honour, by truſting to it for his perſonal ſafety, effectually gained their eſteem, and ſome time after a deputation of their Chiefs waited on him. By a variety of attentions, by little preſents, and acts of perſonal kindneſs, he ſo ſubdued their ferocious ſpirits, that they promiſed to deſiſt entirely from their uſual depredations; and returning to their families and their people, the whole body became earneſt to be perſonally introduced to this humane and benevolent ſtranger. Mr. Cleveland had by this time digeſted his plan, which he brought forwards by degrees, and whatever he propoſed they inſtantly agreed to.

He ſent preſents to their wives, and wherever he ſaw he careſſed their children, decorating them with beads; and to their Chiefs he preſented medals, as a mark of his friendſhip, and as a reward for their improving civilization. At length, when he found them prepared for the accompliſhment of his plan, he ordered cloaths to be made, like thoſe of the Seapoys in the Company's ſervice for a few, he furniſhed them with firelocks, and they became regularly drill'd. Vain of their newly acquired knowledge, theſe new ſoldiers ſoon imparted the enthuſiaſm to the reſt of the nation, who earneſtly petitioned for the ſame diſtinction. Thus, at their own requeſt, a battalion was formed for the preſervation of good order, and in leſs than two years, he had a fine corps of theſe people embodied, for the expreſs purpoſe of preſerving from injury the very country that had for centuries before been the ſcene of their depredations. A camp was formed for a corps of a thouſand men, three miles from Bauglepoor, where their families reſided with them, and where ſtrict military diſcipline was obſerved. Thus the ingenuity, addreſs, and humanity of one man effected, in the ſpace of little more than two years, more than could even have been hoped for from the utmoſt exertions of military ſeverity.

After leaving the village of Barkope, which is nearly in the centre of the Jungleterry, and travelling through the flat country, croſſing a ſmall river, we entered the hills, which are covered with wood, and from the ſummits of ſeveral had beautiful and extenſive proſpects, moſtly diverſified by the meandering of the Ganges, and by the varied face of the country, to a great extent, from the eastern shore.

Though the space which we travelled in this route was not great, the serpentine road, the closeness of the woods, and, in many places, the extreme steepness of the hills occasioned considerable heat and fatigue. On the second day of our journey, we arrived at the village on the hill, where the ceremony was to take place: here Mr. Cleveland was received with every mark of respect and affection by the chiefs who were already assembled, and even the women and the children contended who should be the most forward in expressing their regard.

They had built a small open hut in the village, purposely for his reception, and the following morning every person in the neighbourhood was collected to be present at the annual sacrifice.

The ceremony took place about nine o'clock. Before a small hut, and about six feet from the ground, was raised a kind of altar made of bamboos. The grand sacrifice was preceded by the decolation of a kid and a cock, the heads of which were thrown upon the altar, and there remained: little attention however was paid to this part of the ceremony by any of the party present. An hour or more afterwards, we were apprised that the principal rite was about to be performed, and we repaired in conſequence, without loſs of time, to the place of rendezvous.

The people had purchaſed a fine large buffaloe, which they had fattened, and were now dragging with ropes, by the horns, towards the ſpot where the kid and the cock had been already ſacrificed. The animal was brought, with much difficulty, to the place of ſacrifice, where the chief of the village attended: he was perfectly naked, except a cloth round his middle, and held a large and bright ſabre in his hand. The place round the altar was ſoon crowded with people; men, women, and children attended, and the young men were all perfectly naked. To prevent the eſcape of the animal, they firſt ham-ſtringed him, and then began the dreadful operation. The chief ſtood on the left ſide of the animal, and with his ſabre ſtriking the upper part of the neck, near to the ſhoulder, muſt have given exquiſite pain to the poor animal, who expreſſed it with great violence, by writhing, bellowing, and ſtruggling with thoſe that held him; indeed, their utmoſt exertions were ſcarcely ſufficient to prevent him from breaking away. This horrid buſineſs continued for the ſpace of more than a quarter of an hour, before the ſpine of the neck was cut through. When the animal fell, the Melchiſadeck of the day ſtill continued his work, and it was ſome time before the head was perfectly ſeparated. Previous to the laſt ſtroke, he ſeemed to pauſe, and an univerſal ſilence reigned: when this was given, he ſtood perfectly erect, and, by raiſing the arm which held the ſabre to the utmoſt extenſion, ſeemed to give the ſignal to the multitude, who ruſh'd in and began ſcooping up the blood of the animal, which had liberally flowed from him on the ground. This they drank up, mixed as it was with the duſt and loam, and beſmeared each other with their hands. Bodies of them ruſhed over bodies, and rolling in confuſed heaps, they appeared like an aſſemblage of demons or bacchanals in their moſt frantic moments. The body was next cut to pieces, and devoured; the head, however, was reſerved, as thoſe of the kid and the cock: ſo various are men in their conceptions concerning what may be moſt acceptable to the Deity. After the completion of this ſacrifice, they retired to their ſeveral habitations in parties, and began the rejoicing of the day, which, indeed, was devoted to univerſal revelling and intoxication; and I could have wiſhed, for the honour of the fair ſex, that theſe latter exceſſes had been confined to the men. After the rites of Bacchus had far exceeded the bounds of temperance, thoſe who were capable of ſuſtaining an erect poſition began dancing, men and women promiſcuouſly; others, in parties, roared out their extravagant joy in ſuch ſtrains, as may be ſuppoſed adapted to the preſent ſtate of the performers; and the night concluded with a dead ſilence.

Mr. Cleveland did not remain long after the performance of the ceremony; we therefore proceeded on our journey back to Bauglepoor, and on the following day arrived at Deogur, a ſmall village, famous for the reſort of Hindoo pilgrims, this being a ſacred ſpot. There are five curious Pagodas here, of perhaps the very oldeſt conſtruction to be found in India. They are ſimply pyramids, formed by putting ſtone on ſtone, the apex is cut off at about one ſeventh of the whole height of the complete pyramid, and four of them have ſmall ornamental buildings on the top, evidently of more modern work, which are finiſhed by an ornament made of copper, and gilt, perfectly reſembling the trident of the Greek Neptune. Theſe Pagodas have each a ſmall chamber in the center of twelve feet ſquare, with a lamp, hanging over the Lingham*. The paſſage to it is exactly of a heighth and width ſufficient to admit one perſon. This chamber can have no light from without, but what enters from the door and through the paſſage.

At Deogur multitudes of pilgrims are ſeen, who carry the water of the Ganges to the weſtern ſide of the peninſula of India. The water is carried in large flaſks or bottles, holding nearly five quarts each, ſuſpended at either end of a bamboo, which reſts upon the ſhoulders. A conſiderable trade is carried on by theſe people, and the price of the holy water bears a proportion to the diſtance of the place where it is ſold from the river.

* The Lingham is the great object of ſuperſtition among the followers of Brahmah, it being the general ſymbol of renovative nature.

Our return was ſo nearly in the direction in which we came, that no opportunity was offered for any new obſervations; indeed this part of the country does not abound in objects of curioſity. In the great famine which raged through Indoſtan in the year 1770, and the ravages of which were particularly felt in every part of Bengal, the Jungleterry is ſaid to have ſuffered greatly. I have underſtood that it was before this time highly cultivated, and filled with induſtrious huſbandmen and manufacturers, and the population was eſtimated at more than eighteen thouſand people. It is, however, at preſent reduced to a few hundreds, great numbers having been cut off by famine, and others having emigrated in ſearch of food. The ſilence that reigns here, owing to this depopulation, ſpreads a melancholy over the mind of the traveller, and for miles together, nothing is heard but the ſcreams of the cormorant, nor is the trace of any footſteps found but thoſe of the wild elephant. On my return to Bauglepoor, converſing on this ſubject with my friend, I mentioned the popular impreſſions that had gone forth at, and after that melancholy period, and expreſſing my feelings on the ſubject, not without ſeverity againſt ſome leading characters, then in Bengal, and who had been accuſed of taking advantage of the public diſtreſs for the accumulation of large private fortunes; he with his uſual candour and regard to juſtice, explained the conduct of certain gentlemen, who had very unjuſtly ſuffered in their character, by malignant inſinuations, and ſhewed me, from the archives of the diſtrict, written documents collected at the time, which convinced me that the gentlemen, who then reſided in public characters at Moorſhedabad, and at Bauglepoor, and other ſurrounding diſtricts, where the famine raged in its utmoſt violence, had taken and employed every means that liberality and benevolence, under the direction of ability, could poſſibly ſuggeſt for the preſervation of the poor, and many of them at the expence of their own private fortunes. I ſhould not have touched upon this ſubject, but from a motive of ſtrict juſtice, as few perſons have had an opportunity of inſpecting the proofs and records which Mr. Cleveland indulged me with a ſight of.

CHAP. VI.

The Author returns to Calcutta—Seized with a dangerous Illneſs—Recovery—Proceeds on a new Tour—Route from Calcutta to Allahabad—Deſcription of the Fort and Town—Cawnpoor—Lucknow, Deſcription of that City—Palace of the Nabob—Journey to Fyzabad and Oud—Deſcription of the City of Fyzabad—Palace of Sujah ul Dowlah—Oud, &c.

AFTER remaining about four months at Bauglepoor, having completed my buſineſs, I proceeded for Calcutta, where I arrived on the 15th of May, 1782, and immediately after proceeded in thoſe works I had undertaken. The extreme heat at this ſeaſon, however, added to an aſſiduous application to my profeſſion, threw me into a violent fever; and, after my recovery from the diſeaſe, I continued very weak for a long time.

IN this ſtate of debility I had it frequently in contemplation to proceed to Europe; but the cool weather returning towards the end of November, my ſtrength and vigour gradually returned with it. I felt all my curioſity revived; and once more reſolved to indulge my inclination to viſit other parts of India. With this view, I explained to the Governor

General my wishes to visit Agra, &c. &c. and I had the honour of receiving his sanction, and that of the Council. On the 10th of January, 1783, I began my journey by land, passing once more through Moorshedabad, Bauglepoor, Mongheir, and Patna, to Benares. As I had not stopped at any of the above places, except Bauglepoor, where I remained only one day, I found myself considerably fatigued by a journey of nearly five hundred miles, in a pallankeen; I therefore determined to rest at Benares, and was happy to receive the civilities of Mr. Markham, the Resident, a gentleman universally known for his liberality and accomplishments.

Having prolonged my stay four days, and finding myself perfectly recruited, I pursued my journey, and arrived at Allahabad on the second day after I left Benares. This is the point of confluence of the two great rivers Jumna and Ganges; and between the eastern boundaries of the Jumna and the western boundaries of the Ganges is the country known by the name of Dooab, or a country lying between two rivers, the whole of which is esteemed very fertile. Immediately at the point is the fort of Allahabad, built entirely of stone, by the great Emperor Acbar; and commanding, from its situation, the navigation of both rivers; a circumstance which ought to make it a place of consequence, although it is now left to ruin. It is built in the old style of fortification, with walls flanked by round and ſquare towers; and that which is called the Agra gate, pointing towards Agra, is very handſome, being ornamented with many ſmall pavilions on the top; and having within the exterior gate two other gates, which were formerly ſecured with portcullies. The fort covers a conſiderable ſpace of ground, and muſt have required a great number of men for its protection. Within the walls of the fort are large areas; in one of which I obſerved a ſmall monument over the tomb of an Engliſh officer; the inſcription, however, was nearly defaced. Theſe areas are now no more than heaps of ruins, chiefly covered with the duſt of the crumbled buildings. This was one of the many fortreſſes that extended nearly in a line from Lahore to Chunar Gur, on the Ganges, all of which were raiſed by Acbar, and muſt have ſecured the empire from the confines of Perſia to the borders of Bengal. Without the fort is what is called the city; conſiſting, however, merely of thatched huts, and with ſcarcely a veſtige of any conſiderable houſe remaining. This place is now in the poſſeſſion of Aſoph ul Dowlah, Nabob of Oud: it was, for ſome time, the reſidence of the preſent Great Mogul, the unfortunate Shah Allum, after his unſucceſsful attack, and his loſs of the battles of Geriah and Buxar, where he attended the late Nabob Sujah ul Dowlah, and on the loſs of which he threw himſelf on the protection of the Engliſh, by whoſe influence and power Allahabad and the adjoining province of Korah were allotted him for his ſupport.

During a ſtay of three days I made ſeveral drawings of the fort, and then proceeded to Cawnpoor, a large military ſtation on the Ganges. This is a cantonment for a brigade, amounting, on the war eſtabliſhment, to ten thouſand men; and may be conſidered as a great encampment, the men living in huts with their families inſtead of tents.

Crossing the Ganges at this place, I continued my progreſs to Lucknow, where I arrived on the 25th of January. The diſtance from Calcutta to this place is commonly ſaid to be, by the route through Benares, nearly nine hundred miles; but this eſtimate is certainly too great. Major Rennell, whoſe authority muſt be conſidered as abſolute, determines it to be 650 miles, by the neareſt road. It is well known that this city is at preſent the capital of the province of Oud, and the reſidence of Aſoph ul Dowlah, the Nabob, who is alſo Vizier of the remaining part of the empire of the Great Mogul. The city is extenſive, but meanly built: the houſes are chiefly mud walls, covered with thatch, and many conſiſt entirely of mats and bamboos, and are thatched with leaves of the cocoa nut, palm tree, and ſometimes with ſtraw. Very few, indeed, of the houſes of the natives are built with brick: the ſtreets are crooked, narrow, and the worſt I have ſeen in India. In the dry ſeaſon the duſt and heat are intolerable; in the rainy ſeaſon the mire is ſo deep, as to be ſcarcely paſſable; and there are a great number of elephants, belonging to the Nabob and the great men of his court, which are continually paſſing the ſtreets, either to the palace, or to the river, to the great danger and annoyance of the foot paſſenger, as well as the inferior claſs of ſhopkeepers. The comforts, the convenience, or the property of this claſs of people are, indeed, little attended to, either by great men or their ſervants; the elephant himſelf is frequently known to be infinitely more attentive to them as he paſſes, and to children in particular.

The palace of the Nabob is on a high bank, near to the river, and commanding an extenſive view both of the Goomty and the country on the eaſtern ſide. A ſmall part of it was raiſed by the late Nabob Sujah ul Dowlah, the father of Aſoph ul Dowlah. It has, however, been greatly extended by the preſent prince, who has erected large courts within the walls, and a durbar, where he receives publickly all perſons that are preſented. This durbar is a range of three arcades, parallel to each other, and ſupported by columns in the Mooriſh ſtyle: the ceiling, and the whole of this, is beautifully gilt, and painted with ornaments and flowers. It is aſcended by ſteps from a flower garden, laid out in the ſame manner as we ſee in Indian paintings, which are all in ſquare plats, in which are planted flowers of the ſtrongeſt ſcent; ſo ſtrong, indeed, as to be offenſive at firſt to the nerves of a European. The exterior of the building is not to be commended: it reminded me of what I had imagined might be the ſtyle of a Baron's caſtle in Europe, about the twelfth century. Close to the palace, divided by a narrow dirty or dusty road, is a garden, lately made by the Nabob, walled round, and at each angle is a grand pavilion, built of brick, and covered with chunam or stucco, and then painted with ornaments, which at a little distance has a rich effect. I have introduced a View of the Palace: on the foreground of the picture is one of the pavilions, and on a high bank is a mosque, with two minarets; and adjoining is a durgaw, or burial place, with a view of the river. The picture from which the print was engraved was painted on the spot.

As at this time Major Brown was appointed on an embassy to Mirza Shuffy Khawn, and was to proceed immediately on his mission through a part of the country which I intended to visit, I wrote to that gentleman, signifying my wishes to accompany him; as I knew that under the protection of his public character I should experience no inconvenience from the suspicions of the people with respect to my pursuits; and as in his answer I found he was not to be at Etawah until the ninth of February, I determined, in the interim, to make a journey to Fyzabad and the ancient city of Oud. I was assisted in this by Mr. Bristow, the then Resident at Lucknow; and immediately on the receipt of Major Brown's letter I set out on my journey, and arrived at Fyzabad on the second day; a distance of forty coss, or eighty English miles, in a south-east direction. As the Resident at Lucknow had writ-

A VIEW of the PALACE of the NABOB ASOPH ul DOWLAH at LUCKNOW.

Engraved by Ja.s Fittler, from a Picture Painted by W. Hodges, R.A.
in the Collection of Warren Hastings Esq.r

London, Publish'd by J. Edwards, Pell Mall, Jan.y 1793.

ten to an officer in the ſervice of the Nabob, reſiding at Fyzabad, I was received at my entrance into the city by a perſon, who was ordered to ſhew the pallankeen bearers to a ſmall houſe in a large garden, which was allotted for my accommodation during my ſtay.

THE city of Fyzabad is of conſiderable extent, and appears to contain a great number of people, chiefly of the loweſt claſs; for the court being removed to Lucknow, drew after it the great men, and the moſt eminent of the merchants, bankers, and ſhroffs, or money-changers. Theſe laſt are perſons in all the towns, and even villages, who make large ſums by their knowledge of the exchange, which in India is in a ſtate of conſtant fluctuation, to the great injury of the poor and the induſtrious.

THE private luxury and vices of the Muſſulman princes too frequently reduce them to a ſtate of real poverty, even with large revenues; and too often they delegate to artful, deſigning, and avaricious characters, the management and concerns of the ſtate, and become virtually the plunderers inſtead of the parents of their ſubjects. Theſe men, eager after their own private gain, and knowing well that their conduct will not bear the blaze of day, connive at any villainy that may be acted by thoſe of inferior degree; many of whom are, indeed, their actual agents. Thus it is that the people at large retain no real regard for their governors, and the natural consequence is, that the princes are frequently left, in the hour of distress, quite destitute of support, and an easy prey to any invader.

In the city of Fyzabad there are remains of many handsome brick buildings. That in which I resided has a large and beautiful pavilion over the gateway or principal entrance. The ascent is by a narrow stair-case, which leads to three open rooms, commanding the whole city on the one side, and on the other the garden and a vast extent of country, with a view of the river Gogra, which is not far distant, and which is here a large river. Opposite the gate is a mosque, (built by the late Nabob) with three domes; the center one is very large. The form of these domes is perfectly that of an egg set on its point: the apparent want of firmness at the base has, however, a very unpleasant effect on the spectator; and however difficult it may have been for the architect to produce, the consideration of this circumstance does not make amends for the evident want of elegance, nay almost of propriety.

Soon after my arrival I was waited upon by a person from the mother of the present Nabob, accompanied with a number of dishes of various curries, and pillaws, for my refreshment after the fatigue of my journey, and compliments in the Moorish style; indeed, so high and dignified, that I could have almost fancied myself tranformed into an

Indian Nabob. After returning my respects in the humblest style, and having taken my repast, which indeed was excellent, (and would have been better, had it been accompanied with a glass or two of good wine instead of water) I proceeded to view the city and the remains of the palace, built by the late Nabob Sujah ul Dowlah. This is a vast building, covering a great extent of ground, having several areas or courts, and many separate buildings in them. In the inner court are the remains of the durbar, or hall of public audience; an elegant building on the same plan as that already mentioned in the palace at Lucknow, but much richer: the painting and gilding greatly gone to decay. There are many other buildings designed for offices, or other accommodations. Within an interior court is a large extent of building, the principal front of which is on the banks of the river; and when it was first raised must have been very handsome. This was the part designed for the domestic habitation of the Nabob. Adjoining are other buildings, designed for the Zananah, and in which are the remnants of the gardens. The grand entrance to the palace is through a large and handsome gate, the superstructure of which was a place of arms, and there is still a guard kept in it. On the top of the gate was the situation of the nobut, (a great drum) which is an appendage of royalty in India, and when beaten is heard over a great city. The nobut is usually beaten at sun-rise and sun-set. Nearly adjoining Fyzabad are the remains of the very ancient city of Oud, which is ſaid to have been the firſt imperial city of Hindoſtan, and to have been built by their hero Kriſhen. In Colonel Dowe's tranſlation of Feritſha's hiſtory, it is mentioned as the capital of a great kingdom, one thouſand two hundred and nine years previous to the Chriſtian Æra; and it is frequently mentioned in the famous Hindoo work in Shanſcrite, (the learned language of the Bramins) the Mahaberet, under the name of Adjudea. Whatever may have been its former magnificence, however, no traces are now left. It is ſeated at preſent on the banks of the Gogra; but, in all probability, many years back was at a conſiderable diſtance from it, it being in a line with Fyzabad; for, not many years ſince, upon the building of the palace, Sujah ul Dowlah is ſaid to have daily offered up prayers that the river might flow nearer it, which it now compleatly does, waſhing the walls of the principal front.* At this place and Fyzabad I remained a few days to complete my drawings, and returned to Lucknow by the ſame route as I came. The country I had paſſed through from Allahabad to Lucknow, and thence to Fyzabad, has the ſame general character, and there are very few elevations to be ſeen in it that are conſiderable. It is in a moderate ſtate of cultivation; in ſome parts better than others; but

* Oud is conſidered as a place of ſanctity, and the Hindoos conſequently perform pilgrimages thither, continually, from all quarters of India.

where it is neglected, it is evidently more from the want of property in the people, than the natural sterility of the country, which, on the contrary, I believe to be capable of producing the finest crops. The villages, of which there are many, some are comfortable in their appearance, and others apparently distressed. After leaving the flourishing district of Benares, I could not help viewing with a melancholy concern the miserable appearance of all the territories which were under the absolute direction of Mussulman tyrants.

CHAP. VII.

Journey to Etaya—Deſcription of that Place—Jeſwontnagur —O'Kraine—Shekoabad—Fyrozabad—Etamadpoor—Shah Dara—Agra—Magnificent Ruins—Arrival at the Camp of the Nabob Mirza Shuffy Khawn—A venerable Chief who had ſerved under Kouli Khawn—Mauſoleum of Acbar—Taje Mahael—Futtypoor Sicri—Fortreſs of Gawlior—Return to Lucknow.

ON the 10th of February I ſet out on my journey to join Major Brown at Etaya. As I travelled by a ſet of pallankeen bearers to the number of fifteen, and which had no relief beyond their own ſet, my ſtages became ſhort; particularly ſo, as I was now encumbered with baggage, carrying with me a tent, and all the articles for cooking, &c. the number of ſervants neceſſary for dreſſing proviſions, &c. makes the train even of an individual conſiderable. On the 13th I arrived at the encampment of Major Brown, his tent being pitched cloſe to the town of Etaya. The road to this place runs weſtward from Lucknow, and the Ganges is croſſed nearly midway, and at this ſeaſon of the year is in many places fordable: there is a fordable ſtream alſo to the weſtward of the Ganges, called Callinuddie, which, however, in the time of the periodical rains is a conſiderable river. The country from Lucknow to Etaya is in a moderate ſtate of cultivation, but the villages are poor. Etaya is ſituated on a very high bank of the river Jumna, the ſides of which conſiſt of what in India is called concha, which is originally ſand, but the conſtant action of the ſun in the dry ſeaſon forms it almoſt into a vitrification. Many parts of the banks are ſixty feet high. On the top, near to the river, are the remains of a fort: the town itſelf is all built on the heights, which, as it approaches the river, is divided into a variety of ſeparate hills by deep ravines, made by the rains. The Jumna is at this place a large river, in which are many iſlands of ſand, that are overflowed in the time of the floods. The town is large, but very wretched, having but two tolerable houſes in it.

On the 15th we moved forward to Jeſwontnagur, ſix coſs from Etaya, or near twelve Engliſh miles. It ſhould be obſerved in this place, that the Indian meaſure of a coſs is leſs than in Bengal, the latter being nearly two Engliſh miles; but in the upper parts of Hindoſtan, ſcarcely more than one and a half, as may be ſeen on the ſcale in the map. The country from Etaya to this place is very little cultivated; the villages are not populous, and the few inhabitants appear very wretched.

On the 16th we halted at O'Kraine, ſix coſs further, almoſt at the termination of the Nabob of Oud's country.

Through the whole of the laſt day's journey I obſerved ſcarcely a ſpot in cultivation; the villages, of which there are ſeveral, were in ruins, and the whole preſented almoſt one uninterrupted ſcene of deſolation. On the laſt day's march we met a few unfortunate people paſſing down into the provinces, in order actually to avoid being ſtarved, begging their way. The ſervants we had brought from Bengal with us appearing clean, healthy, and chearful, perhaps rendered the appearance of theſe poor people the more wretched.

On the 17th I arrived at Shekoabad, which takes its name from Dara Sheko, the eldeſt and moſt unfortunate ſon of the Emperor Shah Iehan, who, in the conteſt for the empire with Aurungzebe, his youngeſt brother, was defeated, hunted down like a wild beaſt, and at laſt taken. When a priſoner, he was ſtripped and ſeated on an elephant, for the deriſion of a conquering army, and was at laſt unmercifully murdered. From O'Kraine to this place there are ſome few ſpots of cultivated ground; and the richneſs and fulneſs of the grain ſufficiently ſhew what the whole of the country is capable of producing, were it in cultivation.

During this day's march our courſe lay through two villages, which were better and cleaner than thoſe we had before paſſed. To the right and the left of our road were many ruined villages; and on every hillock, or riſing ground, are mud ſorts, or their ruins. This town (for, on the compariſon with what we had paſſed ſince leaving Etaya, it may be ſo called) has a conſiderable number of people, and the adjacent ground is in cultivation. I found here the remains of a hunting ſeat, built by Dara Sheko, and a tank belonging to it: from the ruins it muſt have been large. Adjoining the tank is a ſmall grove of palm and other trees; but, except theſe, there are no trees in the neighbourhood; nor is there any water but from a few wells, and the abovementioned tank, which was nearly dry when I ſaw it. There are conſiderable remains of other buildings, in and about the town, ſome of them apparently on a large ſcale.

We continued our route, for ſix coſs, to Fyrozabad, which is a conſiderable village. Between Shekoabad and Fyrozabad are a few ſpots of cultivated ground. This village takes its name from the Purgunnah, which is a ſmall diſtrict within a larger: it was at this time in the hand of a Goſine, or Hindoo Religious; and as the ſpirit of the Hindoo government is favourable to agriculture in the higheſt degree, this ſpot appeared a perfect garden. It muſt, indeed, be obſerved, that although the Hindoo governors or proprietors, from the principle of avarice, may ſometimes diſtreſs, they do not deſtroy the endeavours of the poor, as the Muſſulmans. For his protection, the Goſine had a camp formed in the neighbourhood, amounting to two thouſand men, well armed, and a ſmall park of artillery, in which I ſaw two fine pieces of battering cannon. The perſons of the men, forming this little army, appeared to me remarkable for their manly beauty and ſtature, moſt of them being upwards of ſix feet in height, and their manners, whilſt I was in their camp, were extremely modeſt and attentive. On the following day we reached Etamadpoor, a diſtance of ſix coſs, but found in our journey that, upon leaving the Purgunnah of Firozeabad, the line was ſtrongly marked by the wild waſte that enſued.

At Etamadpoor is a ſmall building in the center of a large tank, the ſides of which are built up with ſtone, as is the center building, and a bridge of ſeveral arches, which communicates with it from the ſide of the tank. Around the whole are large mounds of earth, formed from the excavations in making the tank. At this time there was but little water in it.

From this place we had a ſight of the ſpires of the once ſplendid and imperial city of Agra.

On the 23d, at the diſtance of five coſs from Etamadpoor, we encamped on the Shah Darah, about a coſs on the eaſtern ſide of the river Jumna, oppoſite the city. The whole of this ſpot, as far as the eye can reach, is one general ſcene of ruined buildings, long walls, vaſt arches, parts of domes, and ſome very large buildings, as the Cuttera, built by the great Shah Heſt Khawn, in the reign of Aurungzebe; here are alſo ſeveral Tombs.

Along the weſtern bank of the river are ſeen the ruined palaces of the great Omrahs, built in the time of Acbar Jehanguire, and Shah Jehan. A little farther, the city of Agra offers itſelf to the eye, with the great fort and palace, and the proſpect is terminated to the ſouth-weſt by that vaſt monument of eaſtern elegance, the Taje Mahel, built by the emperor Shah Jehan.

This ſpot takes its name from Dara, a tent, and Shah, king or ſovereign, being the ſpot where the emperor's tent was firſt fixed, when he made his progreſs from Agra to the eaſtern provinces of the empire. It being the general cuſtom, from the time the dynaſty of the Moguls was fixed in India, under Acbar, that the emperor ſhould take the field in the ſummer months, with a large army, attended by the whole court, the bankers, and the artiſans, &c. Thus the camp became a great city under tents, and each trade had its ſeveral quarter allotted to them, the emperor's tent being in the center of the whole, ſurrounded by thoſe of the great officers of ſtate.

On the 24th Major Brown was waited upon by Araſiab Khawn, an Omrah of high rank, from the Nabob Mirza Shuffeh Khawn, who lay encamped three coſs to the north-

A VIEW of AGRA taken from the SOUTH WEST.

Engraved by J. Walker from a Picture Painted by W. Hodges, R.A. in the Collection of Warren Hastings Esq.r

London. Published by J. Edwards, Pall Mall, Jan.y 1.st 1793.

weſt of Agra, and to whoſe camp we proceeded, croſſing the Jumna, and paſſed through a part of the city of Agra. On the following day we pitched our tents to the eaſtward of the Nabob's encampment, in a garden walled round, and which formerly was adorned with very conſiderable buildings, now in ruins; this was a work of Acbar for the accommodation of one of his daughters.

The camp of Mirza Shuffeh extended over a great ſpace of ground, and more reſembled a great city than a camp, having ſhops of every denomination, retaining in part the character of the armies of the great emperors, only without their ſplendor. The camp was ſaid to contain forty thouſand men; but it appeared to me that the number was greatly exaggerated. This, however, ſhould be added, that every ſoldier, and every tradeſman and artificer, had his family with him. In the park of artillery were forty-two pieces of cannon of various calibers. Some of the largeſt guns were French pieces, and very fine ones; but the greater number were very indifferent, the metal much corroded, and the carriages rotten. It is not improbable that the tent of the Nabob might have been formerly an imperial one, being of crimſon velvet, embroidered in many parts with gold, and lined with ſilk. It was, however, much torn and moth-eaten, and had therefore no very ſplendid appearance.

A few days after our arrival, I attended Major Brown to the Durbar of the Nabob, where we found the principal commanders, amongſt whom were ſeveral old Perſian Chiefs, with beards depending to their girdles, and countenances of great dignity. One of the hoary Chiefs, I found by his converſation, had attended Nadir Shah, or Thomas Kouli Khan, when he made his famous expedition into Hindoſtan, in the year 1739, and had remained in India ſince that time. The old ſoldier's eye appeared in a flame when he mentioned his name, at the recollection of the actions and victories he had aſſiſted at, or been witneſs to, under his former commander. After the ceremony of reception, which was by touching the turban with the right hand, without riſing from their ſeats, we were deſired to ſit, for which purpoſe there were old faſhioned chairs brought, which had formerly been rich in carved work and velvet, but were now greatly injured by the hand of time; otter and roſe-water were handed round, as a mark of diſtinction. The Nabob Mirza Shuffeh ſat in the center of a ſemicircle, ſurrounded by his Chiefs, with an innumerable crowd of ſervants ſtanding behind. After remaining about half an hour, we retired. This was a viſit of ceremony, and the buſineſs of Major Brown's miſſion was not entered upon for many days afterwards, for, amongſt theſe people, delay ſeems a ſettled principle of etiquette.

Whilst we lay encamped at this place, I made daily excurſions to Agra and the neighbourhood, the weather at this ſeaſon greatly favouring my purſuits. Our journeys were ſhort, and were begun frequently between five and ſix in the morning, ſometimes earlier. I had the whole day for my ſtudies. The climate at this ſeaſon is delightful, the mornings clear and very cold, frequently froſty, in ſo much, that I have ſeen ſeveral tanks frozen entirely over; but in the middle of the day we generally found it very hot. I paſſed moſt of my days at Agra, making drawings either of the great fort or other buildings, moſt of which lay in ruins.

THE city of Agra is ſituated on the ſouth ſide of the river Jumna, which at this place is not fordable, and riſes immediately from the water, extending in a vaſt ſemicircle. It is ſuppoſed to be a place of high antiquity. The preſent city, however, was raiſed by the emperor Acbar, about 1566, and named from him Acbarabad, and was the principal ſeat of his government. The fort, in which is included the imperial palace, is of vaſt extent. A view of the fort is given, and is ſuch as will afford a general idea of the building and its ſituation. It is conſtructed of a red free ſtone, and it would appear to have been very ſtrong, when firſt raiſed. It originally had a double wet ditch, of great width and depth, and well ſupplied from the river. The fort was an iſland, formed by three ditches; one face of it, that to the eaſtward, was waſhed to the foot of the walls by the river. The outer ditch is now totally ruined, the high road going through it, as may be obſerved in the Plate. The inner ditch is very bad in many places, and in ſeveral is quite dry. The city was encircled by a wall and towers at a bow-ſhot diſtance from each other.

Shah Jehan, the grandſon of Acbar, diſliking the ſituation of Agra, from the exceſſive heats to which it was expoſed in the ſummer months, and deſirous to raiſe a metropolis which ſhould bear his own name, built a great city adjoining the old one of Dehli, and named it Jehanabad; but the name, like the empire, is now nearly loſt. To people his new city, he is ſaid to have tranſported thither one half of the people of Agra, to the amount of upwards of five hundred thouſand. The ruins that immediately enſued in Agra, rendered it neceſſary to erect, for the ſecurity of the people, another wall, forming a part of a circle within the old one; and this wall was built by Joy Singh, a Hindoo Raja in the ſervice of the emperor Aurungzebe.

The whole ſpace between theſe two walls is one maſs of ruins. The inner wall is but in indifferent repair, and within it is eaſy to diſcern that it is chiefly compoſed from the ruined buildings, except, indeed, towards the Dehli gate of the fort, where is the great Musjüd or Moſque, built of red ſtone, but greatly gone to decay. Adjacent to this ſpot is the Choke, or Exchange, which is now a mere ruin; and even the fort itſelf, from its having frequently changed its maſters, in the courſe of the laſt ſeventy years, is going rapidly to deſolation. It was taken by Colonel Polier, when that gentleman was in the ſervice of the Nabob Zoolfeccar ul Dowlah, better known by the name of Nedjif Khawn. In the eaſtern front of the fort was the imperial reſidence, built of white marble, covered on the top with plates of copper gilt, which to this day retain their full luſtre, and at no great diſtance there is a Moſque, built of the ſame beautiful materials, with copper ornaments and gilt. It was impoſſible to contemplate the ruins of this grand and venerable city, without feeling the deepeſt impreſſions of melancholy. I am, indeed, well informed, that the ruins extend, along the banks of the river, not leſs than fourteen Engliſh miles.

THE palace of Dara Sheko, built by that prince, includes an extent of ground not leſs than the ſquare of Lincoln's-inn fields. It is dangerous even to walk among theſe ruins; for at every ſtep, unleſs great care is taken, the paſſenger is liable to ſink through holes into the covered vaults, which are now the habitation of dangerous reptiles. The ſtreets in this city are very narrow, and evidently not laid out on any well directed plan. I went once to a Hummaum, or bath, which had formerly belonged to the palace of one of the great men of the court, as was plain from the expences that had been laid out on it; being lined with the fineſt coloured marbles, with many pieces of lapis lazuli introduced amongſt the ornaments, which were very beautiful, in the Mooriſh ſtyle, compoſed of moſaic and flowers; the imitations of the latter, I muſt add, were remarkably good.

AT the diſtance of three coſs, or a little more, from Agra, on the great high road leading to Dehli, at a place called

Secundrii, ſtands the tomb of the emperor Acbar. This enormous building is ſeated in a garden, regularly planted both with foreſt and fruit-trees, and many flowering ſhrubs, and walled round, which is ſuppoſed to contain a ſpace of upwards of twenty Engliſh acres. The monument is raiſed in the center of the garden; it is a ſquare building, with gates in the center on each ſide, and great pavilions at the angles and over the gates: it conſiſts of five ſeveral ſtories, which gradually diminiſh with pavilions at each angle. The domes of the ſeveral pavilions are of white marble, the reſt of the building is of red ſtone, in parts intermixed with white marble. The fifth or upper ſtory is entirely of white marble, and has a range of windows running round each ſide, which are fret work, cut out of the ſolid ſlab. The pavilions that finiſh this ſtory are likewiſe of marble; theſe have been greatly damaged, as I was told, by lightning, and by an earthquake. One of the pavilions is quite gone, and the domes of the others are greatly injured. The inſide of this upper ſtory is curiouſly inlaid with black marble, expreſſive of certain paſſages from the Koran; and I was informed by a critic in Perſian writing, that it is in the moſt perfect ſtyle. On each ſtory of this building are large terraſſes, which, in the times of the emperors Jehanguire and Jehan, had coverings of gold cloth, ſupported by pillars of ſilver. Under the ſhade of theſe awnings the mollahs or prieſts of the religion of Mahommed converſed with men of learning.

The principal entrance is by a grand gate leading to the garden; the front highly ornamented with mosaics of different coloured marbles, inlaid in copartments. On either side the center are two stories of pointed arches, and large recesses; in the upper story is a door in the center, and a window over it, with a ballustrade in front; the lower recesses have one window in each. In the center is one vast pointed arch; and this part of the building rises very considerably above the side over the two stories which have been just described. On the top, and somewhat behind the front of this part of the building, raised on square columns, are two sarcophagi of black marble; and two others immediately behind the back front of the gate, answering to those in the principal front. At each angle of the gate (this building being an oblong square) are minarets of white marble, rising to a great heighth, in part fluted; above the flutes, half way up the minarets, are ballustrades; and there is likewise one near the top. These minarets were formerly crowned with open pavilions, and finished with domes, which have long since been destroyed. In these minarets are staircases, leading to the two balconies that surround them. A large print, by that excellent artist Mr. Brown, has been engraved and published from a picture of this gate, which gives a more perfect idea of the grandeur of it than words are able to express. Through this gate we pass into a vast open hall, which rises in a dome nearly to the top of the building. This hall was, by the order of the Emperor

Jehanguire, the ſon of Acbar, highly decorated with painting and gilding; but in the lapſe of time it was found to be gone greatly to decay; and the Emperor Aurungzebe, either from ſuperſtition or avarice, ordered it to be entirely defaced, and the walls whitened. From this hall, through a ſimilar arch to that in the front, we deſcend into the garden; and the whole of the tomb diſplays itſelf through an avenue of lofty trees. This avenue is paved with ſtone: in the center is a large ſquare baſon, which was formerly filled with water, but was quite dry when I ſaw it. In the center of the baſon was a fountain, the pipe only remaining: the ſupply of water, indeed, had apparently been conſiderable here, for all through the middle of the avenue, and on either ſide, we obſerved channels, which muſt have been deſigned for aqueducts, but which were then dry. At ſome ſmall diſtance from the principal building riſes a high open gate, entirely of white marble, of exquiſite beauty.

A BLAZING eaſtern ſun ſhining full on this building, compoſed of ſuch varied materials, produces a glare of ſplendour almoſt beyond the imagination of an inhabitant of theſe northern climates to conceive; and the preſent ſolitude that reigns over the whole of the neglected garden, excites involuntarily a melancholy penſiveneſs. After viewing this monument of an Emperor, whoſe great actions have reſounded through the world, and whoſe liberality and humanity were his higheſt praiſe, I became deſirous of ſeeing even that ſtone which contained his crumbling remains. There was an old Mollah who attended, and had the keys of the interior of the building, (which is ſtill held in veneration) and who obtains a precarious ſubſiſtence by ſhewing it to the curious traveller. The inſide of the tomb is a vaſt hall, occupying the whole ſpace of the interior of the building, which terminates in a dome; a few windows at the top admit a "dim religious" light, and the whole is lined with white marble. In the center the body is depoſited in a ſarcophagus of plain white marble, on which is written, in black marble inlaid, ſimply the name of

ACBAR.

FROM the ſummit of the minarets in the front a ſpectator's eye may range over a prodigious circuit of country, not leſs than thirty miles in a direct line, the whole of which is flat, and filled with ruins of ancient grandeur: the river Jumna is ſeen at ſome diſtance, and the glittering towers of Agra. This fine country exhibits, in its preſent ſtate, a melancholy proof of the conſequences of a bad government, of wild ambition, and the horrors attending civil diſſentions; for when the governors of this country were in plenitude of power, and exerciſed their rights with wiſdom, from the excellence of its climate, with ſome degree of induſtry, it muſt have been a perfect garden; but now all is deſolation and ſilence. Surrounding the monument of Acbar are many tombs; ſome of them very beautiful: moſt probably they cover the remains of certain branches of his family. The traditionary report is here, that they are the tombs of his wives.

On the high road from Agra to Dehli there are many ſmall buildings, the form of which is a ſquare pedeſtal, upon which riſes a cone, to the heighth of about eight feet. In this cone there are a great number of ſquare niches, in which were placed the heads of malefactors, in terrorem. Theſe likewiſe ſerved the purpoſe of marking the coſs diſtances on the road: many of them are now broken down and covered in the duſt.

To the ſouth-eaſt of the city of Agra is a beautiful monument, raiſed by the Emperor Shah Iehan for his beloved wife Taje Mahel, whoſe name it bears, and is called, by way of eminence, the Taje Mahel. It now ſtands two miles from the city, though formerly it joined it. Adjacent to this monument there was a great bazar, or market for the richeſt manufactures of India, and of foreign countries,* compoſed of ſix courts, and encompaſſed with great open porticoes; but ſcarcely a veſtige of this building is now remaining. The Taje Mahel riſes immediately from the river, founded on a baſe of red free-ſtone, at the extremity of which are octagon pavilions, conſiſting of

* See Tavernier

three ſtories each. On the ſame baſe are two large buildings, one on either ſide, and perfectly ſimilar, each crowned with three domes of white marble; the center dome conſiderably larger than the others. One of theſe buildings is a musjiid, or moſque; the other was deſigned for the repoſe of any great perſonage, who might come either on a pilgrimage to the tomb, or to ſatisfy a well-directed curioſity. On this baſe of free-ſtone (having a platform at leaſt of twenty-five feet in breadth) another reſts of white marble, of a ſquare form, and which is about fourteen feet high; the angles are octagon, from which riſe minarets, or vaſt columns tapering upwards, having three ſeveral galleries running round them, and on the top of each an open pavilion, crowned with a dome. Theſe minarets too, I ſhould have remarked, are of white marble, and contain ſtair-caſes which lead to the top. From this magnificent baſe, like thoſe already deſcribed, riſes the body of the building, which has a platform ſimilar to the above. The plan of this is octagon; the four principal ſides oppoſed to the cardinal points of the compaſs. In the center of each of the four ſides there is raiſed a vaſt and pointed arch, like that deſcribed in the gate of the tomb of Acbar; and the top above this arch riſes conſiderably higher than the other parts of the building. Thoſe faces of the building which form the octagon on either ſide the great arches, have two ſtories of pointed arches, with receſſes, and a low balluſtrade in front; the ſpandels above the arches are greatly enriched with different coloured marble inlaid: the heads of the arches within the receſſes are likewiſe moſt highly enriched in the ſame manner: within the ſeveral arches running round the building are windows, formed by an open fret-work in the ſolid ſlab, to give light to the interior of the building. From behind this octagon front, and riſing conſiderably higher, are four octangular pavilions, with domes. From the center of the whole, riſing as high as the domes of the pavilions, is a cone, whence ſprings the great dome, ſwelling from its baſe outwards conſiderably, and with a beautiful curve finiſhing in the upper point of the cullus, on which reſt two balls of copper gilt, one above the other: above the balls is a creſcent, from the center of which a ſpear head terminates the whole. Each face of this building is a counterpart to the other, and all are equally finiſhed.

WHEN this building is viewed from the oppoſite ſide of the river, it poſſeſſes a degree of beauty, from the perfection of the materials and from the excellence of the workmanſhip, which is only ſurpaſſed by its grandeur, extent, and general magnificence. The baſeſt material that enters into this center part of it is white marble, and the ornaments are of various coloured marbles, in which there is no glitter: the whole together appears like a moſt perfect pearl on an azure ground. The effect is ſuch as, I confeſs, I never experienced from any work of art. The fine materials, the beautiful forms, and the ſymmetry of the whole, with the judicious choice of ſituation, far ſurpaſſes any thing I ever beheld.

It was the intention of the royal founder to have erected on the oppoſite ſhore a ſimilar building, for his own interment, and to have joined them by a marble bridge. This magnificent idea was fruſtrated by ſickneſs, and by the ſubſequent diſputes concerning the ſucceſſion between his ſons, and at laſt by his own impriſonment by Aurungzebe.

The garden, in which the Taje Mahel is ſituated, is entered from the oppoſite ſide, through a large and handſome gate of red free-ſtone, whence proceeds a large flight of ſteps into the garden. From the top of the ſteps the center part of the middle building is viewed through an avenue of cypreſs and other trees mixed: the avenue is paved with ſtone, in the middle there are copartments, or beds of flowers, with fountains at equal diſtances; four of the moſt magnificent of which are ſituated about half way up the avenue, and riſe from a ſquare baſe of white marble. Theſe, as well as the others, are ſupplied by a reſervoir without the building, which is filled from the river by pumps. The fountains are yet in tolerable repair; they were played whilſt I was there; and the garden is ſtill kept in decent order, the lands allotted for the ſupport of the building not being wholly diſmembered from it. The center building is in a perfect ſtate; but all thoſe which ſurround it bear ſtrong marks of decay. Several Mollahs attend the mofque here at the hours of prayer, and appear the moft orderly and decent that I have feen among the Mahomedans; extremely attentive to ftrangers, and affiduous to fhew and explain every part of it. The infide of the great building is of white marble, with many ornaments of flowers beautifully carved. The tomb is in a chamber below, and the body of Taje Mahel lies in a farcophagus of white marble, under the center of the building. Clofe to it is a fimilar one, containing the body of her hufband Shah Iehan. Thefe farcophagi are perfectly fimilar to thofe in the tomb of Acbar.

THE garden and the furrounding buildings cannot occupy a fpace more than equal to one half of that of the Emperor Acbar, at Secundrii. Tavernier mentions, that he was witnefs to the beginning and the finifhing of this building, which employed upwards of twenty thoufand men conftantly at work for a term of twenty-two years. The free-ftone was obtained in the neighbourhood, but the marble was brought from Kandahar, the eaftern province of Perfia, by land carriage, a diftance of not lefs than fix hundred miles by the road. The expence is faid to have amounted to little lefs than one million fterling.

ON the third of March the Nabob's camp moved clofe to Secundrii, where we remained until the fifteenth, when we removed to Gougaut, feven cofs from Agra. Here the

A WOMAN of HINDOSTAN.

MULLAH or MUSSELMAN PRIEST.

Engraved by P. W. Tomkins, from a Drawing made from the Life, by W. Hodges R.A.

London Published by J. Edwards, Pall Mall, Jan 1 1793.

water was very bad, being ſtrongly impregnated with nitre, and the ſurface of the ground was covered with that ſalt. On the twenty-ſecond we encamped near the ſmall village of Krowley, five coſs to the weſtward of Gougaut, on a very extenſive plain, which was poorly decorated with a few ſcattered trees, and bounded by ſome low hills ſtretching to the eaſtward. In theſe hills I found conſiderable quarries of red free-ſtone, the ſame with that of which the fort of Agra is built. The ground was very little cultivated in theſe parts: the ſoil is looſe and light.

I FOUND the heat about this time exceſſive, and it was ſoon much increaſed by the ſetting in of the hot winds from the weſtward. The water through the whole of this part of the country is very bad, from the ſalt-petre.

ON the 23d we encamped near the town of Futtypoor Sicri. The country here reſembled, in moſt reſpects, that which we had juſt paſt. It is an immenſe plain, bounded to the ſouthward by a range of hills; not a ſhrub was to be ſeen; and the heat ſtill continued to increaſe. The ſoil, I obſerved was light, and almoſt as fine as hair-powder. It is impoſſible to deſcribe the diſagreeable effects which this circumſtance produces, when this fine duſt is taken up by the hot winds from the weſtward: the indifferent water too, with which the whole country abounds, muſt neceſſarily render the ſituation unhealthy.

I WAS much entertained, during our ſeveral marches, by the variety of characters I ſaw; the people of the bazar (the market) with their wives and children; the cavalry, who were continually manifeſting their dexterity, in the oriental manner, by ſetting off their horſes in full ſpeed, firing behind, as if purſued by an enemy, and then inſtantaneouſly ſtopping, and flying back with the ſame velocity as they advanced, to the great terror of the poor people in their way. Their adroitneſs in the management of their horſes is, indeed, wonderful; though, from the appearance of the animals, one would doubt whether they were able to move five miles.

To theſe I may add the majeſtic movements of the elephants; not only of thoſe which carried the great men, but of thoſe with the heavy baggage. The appearance, indeed, of the whole army, with the camels, artillery and baggage cattle, formed a ſcene highly gratifying to the mind, entirely new to a European, of ſingular variety, and even ſublime. I could not, however, but obſerve the great apparent want of order in the line of march; not that my knowledge of the military art was ſufficient to qualify me for paſſing a decided judgment; but the order I had ſeen in the camp under Sir Eyre Coote, in the Carnatic, and when thoſe troops marched towards the enemy, gave me very different impreſſions from that which was now before me.

The town of Futtypoor Sicri, which lay under the hills I have before mentioned, is confiderable, and the country immediately near it is in tolerable cultivation. On the fummit of the higheft hill is a large mofque, which was built by Acbar. The building is in a high ftyle of Moorifh architecture. The afcent from the foot of the hill is by a flight of broad fteps, extending to the principal entrance, which is through a portal of great magnificence. After this we enter a large fquare, paved throughout, in which is the mofque, and round the fides are apartments for the different priefts. At the foot of the hill on which the mofque is fituated are the remains of the palace, occupying a great extent of ground. The palace is in total ruin, not a fingle apartment remaining; and the only part which ferves to give any idea of its former beauty is the principal gate. At the back of the hills on which the mofque and palace are built, was a lake, formed by great mounds of earth, artificially raifed to keep in the water, on which, when the palace was inhabited, a number of fine boats were kept of every defcription, for the entertainment of the Imperial Family. The boundaries and banks of the lake are now only to be traced, many parts of it being not only quite dry, but in actual cultivation. Throughout this part of the country the water is very bad, except at the mofque, where it is quite the contrary, the wells being funk confiderably lower than ufual, in fact, below the depth where the falt-petre is generated. While we continued here our feelings informed us of a confiderable increafe in the heat of the weather, in the courfe of a few days.

We remained at Futtypoor Sicri until the twenty-ſixth, when the camp moved to Siedpoor, about ſeven coſs, or a little more. Here we found the face of the country greatly altered; we marched through a territory in many parts well cultivated: to the S. W. of the village it is, indeed, extremely beautiful, being varied with hills, the vallies and plains between which were in fine cultivation. The village itſelf had been but a few months before plundered and burnt, and all the inhabitants maſſacred, by Mahommed Beg Khawn, one of thoſe chiefs who diſputed for the ſovereignty under the Great Mogul, on the death of Nudjiif Khawn, and who, a ſhort time after, aſſaſſinated with his own hand, in a friendly meeting, the chief of this army, Mirza Shuffy Khawn; and for theſe and many ſimilar crimes ſuffered death, by the order of Madajee Scindia, the Mahratta chief.

We experienced great inconvenience about this time from the hot winds, as the reader may well conceive, when he is informed that, in the middle of the day, Farenheit's thermometer ſtood in the ſhade at 106. The great quantities of ſand alſo raiſed by the wind prevented us from ſeeing the ſun ſet for many days, the atmoſphere for many degrees above the horizon being totally obſcured by the floating maſſes of ſand. During my ſtay at Siedpoor there were ſeveral ſtorms of wind only; ariſing in the north-eaſt quarter, and veering about until it ſettled in the ſouth-weſt. The country people call them aundees, and typhawns; but while they rage they may well be called hurricanes; deſtroying every thing in their courſe, and being accompanied with ſuch quantities of duſt, as to have the appearance of a moving cavern approaching to overwhelm the affrighted ſpectators. In one of theſe ſtorms of wind not a ſingle tent in the whole camp was left ſtanding. The duſt raiſed by the ſtorm approaches with a wave-like motion, and affords a clear idea of thoſe tempeſts which are ſaid to happen on the plains of Arabia and in Africa, and which are ſo admirably deſcribed by Lucan; and after him by Mr. Addiſon:

Sudden th' impetuous hurricanes deſcend,
Wheel through the air, in circling eddies play,
Tear up the ſands, and ſweep whole plains away.
The helpleſs traveller, with wild ſurprize,
Sees the dry deſert all around him riſe,
And, ſmother'd in the duſty whirlwind, dies.

THE reader will perhaps have pleaſure in comparing theſe with the following lines of Thomſon:

Strait the ſands,
Commov'd around, in gathering eddies play:
Nearer and nearer, ſtill they dark'ning come;
Till, with the general all-involving ſtorm
Swept up, the whole continuous wilds ariſe:
And, by their noon-day fount dejected thrown,
Or ſunk at night in ſad diſaſt'rous ſleep
Beneath deſcending hills, the caravan
Is buried deep.

My intentions of visiting Dehli were frustrated by the movements of the army under Mirza Shuffy Khawn; and as no probability appeared of reaching that capital under the sanction of Major Brown's embassy, and the country being over-run by two hostile armies, as well as by marauding parties from each, and invaded by the Sciks from the province of Lahore, I was obliged in prudence to direct my course towards Gwalior. I therefore sent off all my baggage under the escort of a party of seapoys, and took my leave of Major Brown on the 28th of April, at night. Added to the evils which I intimated above, the whole country was at this time infested by bands of robbers; and during the march of my small party they were attacked by a considerable body of horsemen, but by the good conduct of the havildar every thing was preserved. On the 29th I arrived at the village of Dohlpoor, and on the following day crossed the river Chumbull, and marched three coss, in a north-west direction, through the worst country I ever saw; full of ravines and deep hollow-ways. As soon as I reached the plain I encamped under the walls of a large mud fort, which had been lately taken from the Rana of Ghod, by Madajee Scindia, the Mahratta chief. The Killidar, or governor, treated my people extremely well, and permitted them to purchase grain and vegetables within the fort, but would not suffer me to enter it.

THE country through which I had lately paſſed was moſt dreary and deſolate, not a blade of verdure to be any where ſeen, and the ſun moſt intenſely hot. On the 1ſt of May I arrived at Nurabad. This is a ſmall town, with an old ſtone fort in it, and a ſtone bridge over a ſmall nullah, (a branch of the Chumbull) conſiſting of ſeven tall and narrow pointed arches: at the extreme of the three center arches are two open pavilions, raiſed upon the bridge, crowned with domes on each ſide; and at the extremes of the other two arches are ſmall cones, all built of the ſame ſtone as the bridge, and finiſhed with little domes: the remaining part of the bridge abuts againſt the banks. On the following day I arrived at Gwalior.

I SHOULD have remarked, that throughout the whole of the above country, which I paſſed in my way from Dohlpoor, there did not appear the ſmalleſt trace of cultivation, nor was there even a hut to be ſeen. The ſeaſon, it is true, was the worſt in the year for the appearance of the country, and the hot winds had ſet in with uncommon violence, which deſtroy every thing in their courſe, like the Angel of Deſolation. Beſides all theſe unfavourable circumſtances, it muſt alſo be remembered, that this is the bordering country, which lies between the fine province of Malwa and that country yet remaining under the dominion of the Great Mogul; and it has conſequently been, ever ſince the eſtablishment of the Mahratta power, the scene of perpetual wars.

The fort of Gwalior is seated on the top of a considerable mountain, rising from a perfect flat country. To the west are some considerable hills, among which is the pass of Narwah, leading to Ougion, the capital of the Malwah country, at present possessed by Madajee Scindia. The rock on which the fort is situated is on every side perpendicular, either by nature or art. At the north-west end is the citadel and a palace, and a chain of seven gates leading to the town at the foot of the mountain. The town, and indeed the whole base of the mountain, is surrounded by a wall; and the place has been generally considered, by Europeans, as the Gibraltar of the East, as well for its natural situation as for the works that have been constructed for its security. The town is large, and contains some few remains of good houses, and a mosque.

During the time of the Mogul government this place was the state prison, where the obnoxious branches of the Royal Family were always confined, and where they were allowed, for their amusement, a large menagerie of beasts, such as lions, tigers, &c. On the top of the mountain, I am told, there are considerable cultivated plains, and a good supply of water; insomuch, that a vigilant and active governor might defend it against almost any number of enemies, who could only attack it from below.

THIS ancient and celebrated fortreſs is ſituated in the heart of Hindoſtan Proper, being about eighty miles to the ſouth of Agra, the ancient capital of the empire, and one hundred and thirty from the neareſt part of the Ganges. From Calcutta it is, by the neareſt route, upwards of eight hundred miles; nine hundred and ten by the ordinary road; and about two hundred and eighty from the Britiſh frontiers. In the ancient diviſion of the empire it is claſſed in the ſubah of Agra, and is often mentioned in hiſtory as the capital of a diſtrict which produced a large revenue. We firſt read of it in the Hiſtory of Hindoſtan, in the year 1008; and, during the two following centuries, it was twice reduced by famine. It is probable that it muſt, in all ages, have been a military poſt of the utmoſt conſequence, both from its ſituation in reſpect to the capital, and from the peculiarity of its ſcite, which was generally deemed impregnable. With reſpect to its relative poſition, it muſt be conſidered, that it ſtands on the principal road, leading from Agra to Malwa, Guzerat, and the Decan; and that near the place where it enters the hilly tract, which advances from Bundelcund, Malwa, and Agimere, to a parallel with the river Jumna, throughout the greateſt part of its courſe. From theſe circumſtances, as well as from its natural and acquired advantages as a fortreſs, the poſſeſſion of it was deemed as neceſſary to the ruling emperors of Hindoſtan, as Dover Caſtle might be to the Saxon and Norman Kings of England.

On the dismemberment of the Mogul empire, Gwalior appears to have fallen to the lot of a Rajah of the Jaut tribe of Hindoos, who assumed the government of the district in which it is immediately situated, under the title of Rana of Gohud or Gohd. Since that period it has changed masters more than once: the Maharattas, whose dominions extend to the neighbourhood of it, having sometimes possessed it, and, at other times, the Rana; but the means of transfer were always either by famine or treachery.

Gwalior was in the possession of Madajee Scindia in the year 1779; at the close of which year the Governor General and Council of Bengal concluded an alliance with the Rana of Gohd; in consequence of which, four battalions of Seapoys, of five hundred men each, and some pieces of artillery, were sent to his assistance, his district being over-run by the Maharattas, and he himself shut up in his fortress of Gohd. The grand object of this alliance was to penetrate into Scindia's country, and finally to draw him from the western side of India, where he then was, attending the motions of General Goddard, who was employed in the reduction of Guzerat. In adopting this measure, the idea of Mr. Hastings was, that when Scindia found his own dominions in danger, he would detach himself from the confederacy, of which he was the principal member, and thus leave matters open for an accommodation with the court of Poonah, the principal ſeat of the Maharatta government; and the event was anſwerable to this expectation. Major, now Colonel Popham, was appointed to the command of this little army, ſent to the Rana's aſſiſtance, and was very ſucceſsful, as well in clearing the country of the enemy, as in expelling them from one of their moſt valuable diſtricts, and keeping poſſeſſion of it. Mr. Haſtings, who juſtly concluded that the capture of Gwalior, if practicable, would not only open the way into Scindia's country, but would alſo add to the reputation of the Britiſh arms, in a degree much beyond the riſque and expence of the undertaking, repeatedly expreſſed his opinion to Major Popham, together with a wiſh that it might be attempted; and founding his hopes of ſucceſs on the confidence that the garriſon would probably have in the natural ſtrength of the place, it was determined that it ſhould be attacked. As the ſucceſs, therefore, of this enterprize is only generally known, I have added the following account of the manner of obtaining poſſeſſion of it, from a letter written by Captain Jonathan Scott, at that time Perſian interpreter to Major Popham, to his brother Major John Scott, who has obligingly permitted the inſertion of it in this work:

"The fortreſs of Gwalior ſtands on a vaſt rock of about four miles in length; but narrow, and of unequal breadth, and nearly flat on the top. The ſides are ſo ſteep, as to appear almoſt perpendicular in every part; for where it was not naturally ſo, it has been ſcraped away; and the height, from the plain below, is from two hundred to three hundred feet. The rampart conforms to the edge of the precipice all round, and the only entrance is by ſteps running up the ſide of the rock, defended on the ſide next the country by a wall and baſtions, and farther guarded by ſeven ſtone gateways, at certain diſtances from each other. The area within is full of noble buildings, reſervoirs of water, wells, and cultivated land; ſo that it is really a little diſtrict in itſelf. At the north-weſt foot of the mountain is the town, pretty large, well built, the houſes all of ſtone. To have beſieged this place would have been vain; for nothing but a ſurprize or blockade could have carried it.

" A TRIBE of banditti, from the diſtrict of the Rana, had been accuſtomed to rob about this town, and once in the dead of night had climbed up the rock, and got into the fort. This intelligence they had communicated to the Rana, who often thought of availing himſelf of it, but was fearful of undertaking an enterprize of ſuch moment with his own troops. At length he informed Major Popham of it, who ſent a party of the robbers to conduct ſome of his own ſpies to the ſpot: they accordingly climbed up in the night, and found that the guards generally went to ſleep after their rounds. Major Popham now ordered ladders to be made, but with ſo much ſecreſy, that, until the night of the ſurprize, only myſelf and a few others knew of it.

"ON the 3d of Auguſt, in the evening, a party was ordered to be in readineſs to march, under the command of Captain William Bruce; and Major Popham put himſelf at the head of two battalions, which were immediately to follow the ſtorming party. To prevent, as much as poſſible, any noiſe in approaching or aſcending the rock, a kind of ſhoes, of woollen cloth, were made for the Seapoys, and ſtuffed with cotton. At eleven o'clock the whole detachment moved from the camp at Reypoor, eight miles from Gwalior, through unfrequented paths, and reached it a little before day-break. Juſt as Capt. Bruce arrived at the foot of the rock, he ſaw the lights which accompanied the rounds moving along the ramparts, and heard the centinels cough (the mode of ſignifying that all is well in an Indian camp or garriſon), which might have damped the ſpirits of many men, but ſerved only to inſpire him with more confidence, as the moment for action, that is, the interval between the paſſing of the rounds was now aſcertained: accordingly, when the lights were gone, the wooden ladders were placed againſt the rock, and one of the robbers firſt mounted, and returned with an account that the guard was retired to ſleep. Lieutenant Cameron, our engineer, next mounted, and tied a rope ladder to the battlement of the wall; this kind of ladder being the only one adapted to the purpofe of fcaling the wall in a body (the wooden ones only ferving to afcend the crag of the rock, and to affift in fixing the rope ladder). When all was ready, Captain Bruce, with twenty Seapoy grenadiers, affembled without being difcovered, and fquatted down under the parapet; but, before a reinforcement arrived, three of the party had fo little recollection as to fire on fome of the garrifon, who happened to be lying afleep near them; this had nearly ruined the whole plan: the garrifon were of courfe alarmed, and ran in great numbers towards the place; but, ignorant of the ftrength of the affailants (as the men fired on had been killed outright), they fuffered themfelves to be ftopped by the warm fire kept up by the fmall party of grenadiers, until Major Popham himfelf, with a confiderable reinforcement, came to their aid. The garrifon then retreated to the inner buildings, and difcharged a few rockets, but foon afterwards retreated precipitately through the gate; whilft the principal officers, thus deferted, affembled together in one houfe, and hung out a white flag. Major Popham fent an officer to give them affurance of quarter and protection; and thus, in the fpace of two hours, this important and aftonifhing fortrefs was completely in our poffeffion: we had only twenty men wounded, and none killed. On the fide of the enemy, Bapogee, the Governor, was killed, and moft of the principal officers were wounded."

A VIEW of the FORT of GWALIOR.

Engraved by W. Byrne from a Picture Painted by W. Hodges R.A. in the Collection of Warren Hastings Esq.r

London, Published by J. Edwards, Pall Mall Jan.y 1. 1793

It is neceſſary to add to this account, that ſome time after, the fort was given up to the Rana of Gohd, who kept poſſeſſion of it until the time of which I am now ſpeaking; the peace being agreed on between the Britiſh Government and Scindia, although not finally ſettled, that chief found himſelf at leiſure to inveſt it once more, and was at this time before the place with ſeventy thouſand men: he, however, only effected its reduction by the treachery of one of the Rana's officers, who admitted a party of the Maharatta troops. A view of Gwalior is given, taken on that ſide where the Engliſh troops eſcaladed, which was near the centre of the length of the mountain.

It would be the height of ingratitude not to make my acknowledgments, in this place, to Meſſrs. Anderſons, who were then in Scindia's camp, forming the treaty of peace and alliance between the Engliſh Company and Madajee Scindia, and which was afterwards ſo ably concluded by thoſe gentlemen, for the uncommon attentions I there received. Mr. Anderſon had ſent an eſcort of Maharatta horſe to Dohlpoor for my protection, which was abſolutely neceſſary, from the then ſtate of the country.

From the fatigue I had undergone, from the violent heats and expoſure to the ſun, in making my drawings, I found myſelf about this time, as indeed I had been for ſome time back, in a very indifferent ſtate of health; nor was I able to ſtir abroad for many days after my arrival at Gwalior: in ſhort, when I was, I was prevented from viſiting the camp of the Maharattas, ſince the peace not being fully adjuſted, many ſuſpicions might have ariſen to retard what was now ſo ardently deſired, theſe people not having the remoteſt idea of any perſon viſiting countries for ſcientific information, in any line whatſoever. After remaining ten days, I therefore determined to purſue my journey, with all expedition, to Lucknow; and accordingly proceeded by Dauk Bearers, and left my ſervants, with my baggage, to follow at leiſure.

I SET off on the 12th, at night, and reached Gohd on the following day, where I ſtopped a few hours to refreſh myſelf: here I found an Engliſhman, who was a watchmaker, but at this time commanded two battalions of the Rana's infantry; he expreſſed himſelf heartily tired of his military career, and a wiſh to return within the Britiſh territory, to his former occupation, as he had made ſome little property in the Rana's ſervice, which he wiſhed to retreat with, but had no means to convey it, not being ſuffered to depart; he therefore requeſted I would take charge of a caſket for him to Lucknow, which I readily did, and delivered it to his friend. Had I, however, foreſeen the diſmal country I was to paſs through, I ſhould have been extremely averſe to this undertaking; for, from the town of Gohd, it is hardly poſſible for the imagination to figure any thing ſo diſmal, duſky, and barren. There were no villages, and ſcarcely a human being to be found, until I arrived near the river Chumbull, the banks of which are very high, and deſcending through deep ravines, in ſome of which are huts: in this part, as a ſtranger paſſes, every now and then a ſavage-like being ſtarts out, completely armed in their way; fortunately, however, the countenance of an European is, in the preſent day, a paſſport. I was two days and a night on this journey from Gwalior to Etaya. The heats, in the middle of the day were extreme, and the bearers, having one day miſſed their way in this ocean of ſand, they ſet me down, and left me, while they went ſome diſtance to a hut to enquire the road. In this ſituation I was for upwards of two hours, when ſome of them returned; and heartily rejoiced I was at the ſight of a human being: it was impoſſible, indeed, to be angry at their long ſtay, when I conſidered what they muſt have ſuffered. On my arrival at Etaya, the ſight of a few green herbs made me conſider it as almoſt a very Eden.

On the 16th, I finiſhed this journey at Lucknow, when the heats and fatigue I had ſuffered brought on a violent dyſentery, and a palpitation at the heart, from which I was long in recovering. Colonel Polier received me with his wonted hoſpitality; and I remained with that gentleman about ten days: my indiſpoſition, however, rather increaſing than abating, his houſe being a large bungelow, * was conſequently very hot, and therefore Colonel Martin, who had a large brick houſe, had the goodneſs to invite me to his, where, by his great and moſt friendly care, and the adminiſtering of proper remedies, I gradually recovered; to him, therefore, I may now ſay I owe the life I at preſent enjoy.

I CANNOT but add, that, independent of this circumſtance, I feel a weight of obligations to that gentleman, for the many and repeated inſtances of his kind and friendly attention. During my ſtay in his houſe I painted ſeveral pictures, among others a large one, a View of the Palace of the Nabob, from which a print has been engraved, which is annexed.

* Bungelows are buildings in India, generally raiſed on a baſe of brick, one, two, or three feet from the ground, and conſiſt only of one ſtory: the plan of them uſually is, a large room in the center for an eating and ſitting room, and rooms at each corner for ſleeping; the whole is covered with one general thatch, which comes low to each ſide: the ſpace between the angle rooms are viranders, or open porticoes, to ſit in during the evenings: the center hall is lighted from the ſides with windows, and a large door in the center; ſometimes the center viranders, at each end, are converted into rooms.

CHAP. VIII.

Departure from Lucknow—Voyage down the River Goomty—Danger from Banditti—Jionpoor—Mausoleum—Sasseram—Mausoleum of Shere Shah—Death of Mr. Cleveland—Arrival at Calcutta—Reflections on the State of the Arts in India—A new Project—Advice to Artists travelling in India.

FINDING myself tolerably recovered, I now determined to return towards Calcutta, and, instead of travelling the same rout by which I came, I resolved to pass by water down the river Goomty. I left Lucknow, therefore, on the 16th of July; and, from the various windings of the river, I did not enter the Ganges (into which the river falls) until the 1st of August.

THE banks of this river are, in most places, very beautiful, and at this season particularly so, having smooth, sloping banks of vegetable earth, and a fine verdure. There are many villages on its banks, between Lucknow and the town of Jionpoor, but less cultivation, than I should have judged, would have been necessary from the apparent population. It is somewhat dangerous to proceed down this river without an escort of the military for protection: near the village of Sultanpoor, there appeared a body of about fifty horse belonging to a famous marauder Rah Sing, who had made himself extremely obnoxious by his depredations. His party watched my boats the whole of one night, within fifty yards of us; the alertness of my Seapoys, however, prevented any attack, and at day-break the party marched off.

Not far from where this river enters the Ganges, stands the fort of Jionpoor, a building of considerable extent, on a high bank commanding the bridge. It is now chiefly in ruins, though formerly, from strength and natural situation, it commanded the country from the Ganges quite to Lucknow: It was built by Sultan Feroz Shah, about the year 1102, and this place at one time was the seat of an empire. Chaja Jehan, Vizier to Sultan Mahummud Shah, during the minority of his son, Sultan Mamood Shah, assumed the title of Sultan Shirki (or king of the East), and took possession of Bahar, and fixed his residence at Jionpoor, where he built the great musjüd or mausoleum, which is still remaining, for the interment of himself and his family. This ruin is a great pyramid in the front, blunt at the top, the apex being cut off; the front is covered with ornaments. Over the center of the building in which are the remains of the tombs, rises a dome, but much below the front of the building which is seen from without; there has also been a square of buildings in the front, as appears by the foundations, which now only remain.

The bridge of ſtone croſſing the Goomty at this place is in tolerable repair, and conſiſts of ſixteen pointed arches; on the top of the bridge are many little ſhops on both ſides built of ſtone. From a Perſian inſcription on the bridge, we find it was founded by Khan Khannah, Vizier to the Emperor Acbar, and Subah of the province of Oud, in the year 1567. The ſound principles upon which this bridge is built, are proved by its having withſtood, for ſuch a length of time, the force of the ſtream, which in the time of the rains is very great. The inundations have been frequently known to riſe even over the bridge, inſomuch, that in the year 1774, a whole brigade of the Britiſh forces paſſed over it in boats. *

The river Goomty falls into the Ganges at a ſmall diſtance below the city of Benares, whence I proceeded direct to Buxar. At this time I alſo determined to make a journey to Saſſeram, twenty coſs inland, the birth-place of the Emperor Shere Shah, to viſit the mauſoleum of that Emperor, and to make drawings of it. This being the ſeaſon of the rains, it was with difficulty I could paſs in my palankeen; in many places the bearers waded above their middle in water, and the whole ground was one continued ſwamp.

I could not but be greatly ſtruck with the grandeur of this monument, riſing from the center of a large ſquare lake, each ſide bounded by maſonry, and deſcending to the water by

* A brigade conſiſts of ten thouſand men.

ſtone ſteps on every ſide, now greatly ruined. I judged, by walking round the lake, and meaſuring it by time, to exceed a mile. The plan of this mauſoleum is a ſquare baſe, riſing from the center of the lake, having at each angle pavilions crowned with domes, and finiſhed with a cullus; from this baſe was a bridge, that, from the ruins now remaining, muſt have conſiſted of ſix pointed arches, which communicated to the ſide of the lake, and on two ſides are a double flight of ſteps to the water; on the baſe is raiſed an octagon building, having three pointed arches in each face, and on each angle are pavilions finiſhed like the former. Somewhat behind this runs an octagon with one window in each ſide, and on the angles, pavilions like the others below; behind this is likewiſe an octagon, ninety-two feet in diameter, and from the extremes ſpring the dome, which is finiſhed on the top by a ſmall pavilion, like thoſe already deſcribed. A great part of the building is now covered with ſhrubs and trees, which have taken root within the ſtones, and promiſe a ſpeedy decay, if not a total overthrow, of this grand pile. The country in the neighbourhood is hilly; and ſurrounding the lake are hills, formed by the excavations when it was firſt made; moſt of theſe are now covered with trees. The inſide of the building is perfectly plain, nor does it appear ever to have had any decorations. The tomb of the Emperor is ſtill remaining in the center, with ſeveral others ſurrounding it, which are thoſe of his children. The dome, like the reſt of the building, is of a fine grey free ſtone, now diſcoloured by age and neglect.

On my return to Buxar, I proceeded to Bauglepoor, where I found my friend Mr. Cleveland on the bed of ſickneſs, which in leſs than three months deprived the Indian world of his valuable life, a loſs irretrievable to his friends, and moſt ſeverely felt by the public.

A constant, and indeed an inceſſant application to public buſineſs, without ſufficient care of a very delicate frame, and poſtponing until it became too late, the expedient of trying a more favourable climate, terminated the mortal exiſtence of this ineſtimable man, who died on board a ſhip, at the mouth of the Ganges, in which he had embarked for the Cape of Good Hope. His remains were brought back in the pilot veſſel that had attended the ſhip, and were afterwards depoſited at Bauglepoor, where a handſome monument was erected to his memory.

I arrived at Calcutta on the 24th of September, after a journey of nine months and fourteen days, through a country which had once been ſubject to the Moguls; the greateſt and the richeſt empire, perhaps, of which the human annals can produce an inſtance, and which was adorned by many really great characters in politics and in arms.

I cannot look back at the various ſcenes through which I paſſed in theſe excurſions, without almoſt involuntarily indulging a train of reflections relative to the ſtate of the arts, under this, as well as under the Hindoo government. The amazing monuments which are ſtill to be found in India, prove the Muſſulman conquerors, to have been well acquainted with the principles of architecture, and at leaſt to have had a taſte for grand compoſition; in painting, on the contrary, they have only exerciſed themſelves in miniature, many of which are highly beautiful in compoſition and in delicacy of colour; their attempts in this art have alſo been confined to water-colours; and they have laboured under a further diſadvantage, the religion of Mahommed prohibiting all reſemblances of animated nature. Whether the Arabs have ever tranſgreſſed the law in this point, I know not; but probably, on account of the remoteneſs of India from the original ſeat of the religion of Mahomed, it may have loſt much of its rigour, and may, therefore, have left the princes of India at more liberty to indulge themſelves in this elegant art.

In ſculpture there are no inſtances of excellence among the Moors, except in the Taje Mahael at Agra, upon which there are flowers carved with conſiderable ability.

The Hindoos appear to me to riſe ſuperior to the Mahommedans in the ornamental parts of architecture. Some of the ſculptures in their buildings are very highly to be commended for the beauty of the execution; they may, indeed, be ſaid to be very finely drawn, and cut with a peculiar ſharpneſs. The inſtance which is produced in this work of a column from the temple of Vis Visha, at Benares, will prove it although cut in free-stone. A similar instance cut in black basalt, in the collection of Charles Townley, Esq. (on which are ornaments similar to those which is referred to above) is a striking proof of their power in this art. This column was brought from Gour, an ancient city, (now totally demolished) situated on the eastern shore of the Ganges, nearly opposite to Rajemahel. I have seen many instances of cast metal statues, relative to Hindoo mythology, that prove their perfect knowledge in the art of casting. These works, as they apply to the religion of Bramah, are both curious and valuable; but, as they are purely mythological, the artists have only considered the symbolical character; without the proper attention, and, perhaps, without a power of giving a perfect beautiful form, such as we see in the Grecian statues.

THE paintings of the Hindoos, as they are, like their sculpture, chiefly applied to represent the objects of their religious worship, are certainly not so perfect as the Moorish pictures, which are all portraits. A constant study of simple nature, it is well known, will produce a resemblance which is sometimes astonishing, and which the painter of ideal objects never can arrive at.

I CANNOT close these pages without mentioning an intention which I entertained, after my last journey, of undertaking another from the Ganges, through the Deccan, to the weſtern coaſt of India; and which I ſhould recommend to the attention of any artiſt who may be induced to viſit India, in future, with intentions ſimilar to thoſe which drew me from my native country. I meant to have commenced my journey at Benares, and finiſhed at Surat. As this is a part of India untrodden by an artiſt, much matter might be collected relative to the ſtate of ancient India, as many of the Rajahs in that part of the country poſſeſs lands handed down from the earlieſt period of the Hindoo records. I muſt think, from what I have ſeen of the Hindoo character, that ſuch a journey might be carried into execution with perfect ſafety, and would add greatly to our ſtock of knowledge relative to the Eaſtern continent.

It is but too true that the expences would be conſiderable, from the neceſſity of being attended by a great number of ſervants; for, as is juſtly obſerved by Mr. Orme, in his ſecond volume, "The different caſts of the Indian religion being appropriated to ſpecific and hereditary vocations, many of them are entirely prohibited from ſervile offices and hard labour; and of thoſe allotted to ſuch occupations, each muſt abide by that alone to which he was born: the huſbandman would be diſhonoured by employing his mattock, excepting in the field he is to ſow; and even lower races have their diſtinctions, inſomuch, that the cooly, who carries a burden on his head, will not carry it on his ſhoulder." The reputation, however, that would neceſſarily attend the completion of ſuch an undertaking, would be more gratifying than whatever wealth might be accumulated in the common track of profeſſional purſuits.

A PAINTER for ſuch purſuits ought neceſſarily to be endowed with three great qualities; a perfect knowledge of his art, and with powers to execute readily and correctly; judgment to chuſe his ſubjects; and fancy to combine and diſpoſe them to advantage. The firſt I muſt ſuppoſe him poſſeſſed of; in the ſecond is included the choice of ſubject, with the knowledge of all the parts neceſſary for ſuch a ſubject; and in the third is included the combination of all the different parts, ſo as to produce a general effect: but the imagination muſt be under the ſtrict guidance of cool judgment, or we ſhall have fanciful repreſentations inſtead of the truth, which, above all, muſt be the object of ſuch reſearches. Every thing has a particular character, and certainly it is the finding out the real and natural character which is required; for ſhould a painter be poſſeſſed of the talents of a Raphael, and were he to repreſent a Chineſe with the beauty of a Grecian character and form, however excellent his work might be, it would ſtill have no pretenſions to reputation as characteriſtical of that nation.

MANY other tours in that intereſting country might be undertaken by the enterprizing artiſt. We know that the whole coaſt of Malabar poſſeſſes pictureſque beauty equal to any country on earth; and how valuable would be the representation of that ſcenery, whether as a natural object, or as connected with the hiſtory of the country, and the manners of the people? Pictures are collected from their value as ſpecimens of human excellence and genius exerciſed in a fine art; and juſtly are they ſo: but I cannot help thinking, that they would riſe ſtill higher in eſtimation, were they connected with the hiſtory of the various countries, and did they faithfully repreſent the manners of mankind.

FINIS.